PRIVACY
AND ITS
INVASION

PRIVACY
AND ITS
INVASION

Deckle McLean

PRAEGER

Westport, Connecticut
London

Library of Congress Cataloging-in-Publication Data

McLean, Deckle.
     Privacy and its invasion / Deckle McLean.
          p.   cm.
     Includes bibliographical references (p.   —   ) and index.
     ISBN 0–275–95335–1 (alk. paper)
     1. Privacy, Right of.   2. Privacy.   I. Title.
     JC596.M34   1995
     323.44'8—dc20   95–9308

British Library Cataloguing in Publication Data is available.

Library of Congress Catalog Card Number: 95–9308
ISBN: 0–275–95335–1

First published in 1995

Praeger Publishers, 88 Post Road West, Westport, CT 06881
An imprint of Greenwood Publishing Group, Inc.

Printed in the United States of America

The paper used in this book complies with the
Permanent Paper Standard issued by the National
Information Standards Organization (Z39.48–1984).

10 9 8 7 6 5 4 3 2 1

For PBM

Contents

Preface

This book explores why privacy is important, has always been important, and can play an instrumental role in most lives. Along the way the book acknowledges the dark side of privacy, teases out the privacy element embedded in some widely recognized problems, and notes the awkward but potentially harmonious relation of privacy to press freedom.

Privacy is a topic of growing awareness and should be because as the century ends privacy is in crisis. The crisis is interior to each of us; we are in conflict; we do not know what to think of privacy and its invasion. The technology used to invade privacy is alarmingly advanced; yet the refinement of data collection and surveillance is not at the core of the problem. If we knew our own minds, we could regulate the technology with clear resolve. But we do not know our minds.

It is not merely that we recklessly divulge private economic information in order to get credit or college financial aid; in addition, we hunger after the ugly private secrets of celebrities, the latest nude pictures of royalty, fallen sports figures, or scions of well-known families, and the wave of sad, banal, but occasionally interesting disclosures provided by those who thereby purchase their moment in the limelight on talk shows. At the same time we wonder how anyone can live in such a fishbowl, and we hope it never happens to us. Sometimes some of us feel a bit uncomfortable, or even guilty, when we find ourselves perusing some of these materials—and enjoying them.

When we contemplate what is bad about life in crowded urban housing developments, we think of crime and the simple want that results from insufficient material possession. Then it occurs to us that the people there get very little privacy. Then, just possibly, it also occurs to us that without privacy children in such developments cannot get their homework done. And then it dawns on us that any society that requires sophisticated mental skills must provide a great deal of privacy; otherwise, no one can learn what is necessary or get their jobs done after they do.

Anyone who has ever been hit with sudden tragic news knows that a person needs quiet moments in which to absorb the shock or in which to break down and recover; yet many people will gawk at a television screen as tape is broadcast of someone undergoing the hammer blow of just such news. Most will be physically unable to avert their attention from the screen, even though they know that something is wrong with pestering a person at such a time.

Privacy. We want it for ourselves; we love to invade other people's. But to accept such selfishness in ourselves is not good enough. We need to do better, to work out an approach or a policy, or at least an individual policy.

The purpose of this book is to identify some of the virtues of privacy, to recognize some of its flaws, and to convince the reader that privacy has been very important for a very long time, and is exceptionally important as the century closes.

_____ Chapter 1 _____

The Difficulty of Privacy as an Idea

Privacy has always been important, but it has always been taken for granted. As a result, very few people have singled it out for attention. It did not seem worth it. This is changing.

Prior to the twentieth century, privacy was a feature of privilege, owned by the wealthy, or a fringe benefit—or curse—of deep rural life. It entered conversation as light observation but not at depth: "They're a private family"; "She hardly needs any privacy at all"; "Leave me alone so that I can work this out in private." Famous philosophers did not address the subject. In fact, philosophers and religious figures everywhere ignored it.

Privacy and its invasion were features of other issues, but were not isolated from these other issues. For example, the droit du seigneur, the medieval European "first night right" under which the feudal lord was entitled to first have sex with a newlywed bride, generated disgruntlement. Yet, the right was terminated because it was an abuse of power, an affront to marriage as an institution, and an insult to lower classes whose power was growing, not because it was an invasion of privacy.

Another example was American slavery. Slavery was wrong in the viewpoints of slaves themselves, abolitionists, and eventually most others; but in the consciousness of slavery's opponents, privacy played no role. To them, slavery was inherently wrong, or wrong as a deprivation of liberty, or as a repudiation of Christian principle, not as a violation of privacy. Yet the invasion of privacy was part of what made slavery so bad. The owner or overseer could extract by torture or intimidation the content of intimate communications, veto or command marriages, take control of children and train or indoctrinate them as he or she wished, use women—or men—sexually without answering for it, frustrate study or learning, maintain surveillance with impunity through informers, or enter a slave's house at any time. Even so, no one thought to challenge slavery as a violation of privacy.

Privacy was also a factor in relationships between social classes. Members of higher social and economic classes could interrupt members of lower classes or meddle in their lives, while members of lower classes could not routinely do the same to members of higher classes. Greater or lesser security in one's privacy was a feature of class difference; but where class became politicized, as by the socialist parties of the late nineteenth and twentieth centuries, the focus was on revoking privilege, ending poverty, or venting anger, not on protecting privacy.

While privacy was then an element embedded in other issues, in the twentieth century it has been pressed forward as a concept that demands independent attention. Probably, a combination of the following forces accounts for the change. First, some methods of violating privacy were refined during the twentieth century: Bureaucratic efficiency grew, and electronic data processing was perfected. Second, because progress was made in addressing such recognized issues as women's inequality, class conflict, caste formation, racial injustice, religious intolerance, local political tyranny, and child labor, privacy itself was left visible in the cleared underbrush. Third, aspirations for privacy increased in the industrially advanced countries as the general level of wealth rose. Many people began to think of themselves as higher in class than they had been and to demand a privilege that higher classes appeared always to have had. Fourth, the principal challenges facing large populations underwent a significant change from gross physical, economic, or political challenges to internal goals, such as self-improvement and service to others.

For example, the twentieth-century movement to increase women's options and revise sex roles was more of a challenge to inner self-improvement than it was an external political challenge. It was quite different, for example, from the late eighteenth-century American challenge to throw off the English yoke. Similarly, the late twentieth-century challenge in the United States, Japan, and Europe to admit persons of other ethnic or racial groups to fully human status in one's own mind was quite different from simply abolishing slavery, withdrawing from Korea, or granting independence to former colonies. Several trends, then, appear to have converted privacy from being a hidden component of other issues into an issue in itself.

Privacy is difficult to discuss for several reasons, one being that the concept of privacy will always be elusive. Another is that privacy has been a target of concentrated attention only for decades, and language has not caught up with the challenge of discussing it. Privacy also presents a valuational problem because many people are not confident that privacy is good, even as they know that they want it.

Privacy will remain elusive as a concept, just as liberty and freedom have remained elusive. Like these other concepts, privacy is a loose political term and subjective values provide part of its load of meaning. A word that represents subjective values can never be precise in meaning. But "privacy" can be as exact a term as "liberty." For example, if the word "privacy" is applied to matters to do with whether others have access to an individual, then privacy is the zone of no access—through information gathering, observation, or physical contact—and invasion of privacy is access that goes beyond a certain point.[1] Persons may differ on where this point should be drawn, but if the word "privacy" is used in this way, it will serve to communicate something tangible.

Similarly, if the word "privacy" is applied to matters relating to commercial exploitation of an individual, then the invasion of privacy is a commercial exploitation that goes beyond a certain point. Commercial exploitation, however, is not the same as access and, as a result, privacy has a somewhat different meaning in this context.

Any discussion of privacy is made more difficult by the newness of the subject. Privacy is about 100 years old as a legal or political issue. The article by Samuel Warren and Louis Brandeis that began the development of American privacy law was published in 1890 in the *Harvard Law Review*.[2] Edward Shils, writing in 1975, described the late nineteenth century as a golden age of privacy, which ended with the arrival of new intrusions.[3] In effect, he has dated privacy as an issue from the close of that golden age. Comparable ideals—liberty, equality, representative government, truth as a defense to libel, free speech and press, religious freedom—took far longer than a century to evolve. Two sets of rights broadly recognized in America for the first time in the nineteenth century, those of women and those of slaves, had been given attention over the course of several thousand years in the Roman world, its Western successor, parallel civilizations, and preceding civilizations.[4] Privacy, however, was brand new as an issue in the nineteenth century.

Glenn Negley, writing in 1966, neatly grasped this newness and also the sea change that accompanies the birth of an issue:

> While the question of privacy has rarely been directly discussed in moral thought, it is not surprising that the problem has been lurking on the fringes of all moral, political, and legal theory, awaiting consideration. It is a historical commonplace that problems often await acknowledgement until circumstantial developments force them upon our attention. After centuries of failure to recognize privacy as a fact pertinent to moral and political speculation, we suddenly find ourselves concerned with the right of privacy as one of the most critical problems of contemporary political and legal analysis. The nature of our social structure as it has developed in the recent past forces us to recognize that the privacy which until now has apparently been casually presumed as an ingredient of

moral action can no longer be presumed but must be specified.[5]

The ability of most people to articulate the nature of privacy
has not caught up with their intuitive understanding that it is
important. In fact, language itself is not yet adequate to the task
of communicating clearly about privacy. Sometimes, very little
meaning is exchanged when the word is used casually. Using
the word "privacy" is a bit like saying someone is "full of bull."
Used in an instant retort to an assertion, "privacy" or "full of
bull" has clear meaning because the term operates in the context created by the assertion. "That's private; it's none of your
business," specifically refers to whatever was just said. So does
"You're full of bull." But in other circumstances, the terms give
only a generalized impression of meaning, unless much explanation is also offered. Two students can share criticisms of a
professor for being "full of bull," and then part company without the vaguest idea of what the other meant, except for know-
ing that the other student did not like the professor and
believed the professor either lied outright in some area or in all
areas, or didn't prepare for some classes or all classes, or offered weak material in some or all topics. Similarly, when "privacy" is used, as in the statement, "He's a private person," we
know only that the person referred to has concerns about his
or her body, territory, or sense of separateness, or that he or
she wishes to hide.

Current usage freights the word "privacy" with broad meaning. American law includes the following under the heading
"invasion of privacy": physical trespass into a space surround-
ing a person's body or onto property under his or her control;
public disclosure of true but embarrassing facts about an individual that this individual wants concealed; lies or reckless
falsehoods that alter a person's public image in ways he or she
cannot control; commercial exploitation of an individual; and,
tampering by government agents in matters related to a person's body, for example, forcing breath tests or stomach pump-
ings upon drunk drivers.[6] The first four are the privacy invasion
torts; the fifth is the constitutional right to privacy.

The word "privacy" is put to broad use generally. It is used to explain why environmental nuisances such as noise or air pollution are offensive. It serves to justify the keeping of a secret, even when the secret doesn't pertain to anything private. It is used to refer to the psychological interior, as when someone seizes a "private moment," a moment of introspection or quiet thought, even though the thought may be about an act of Congress or some equally public matter. It is used in reference to conspiracies of silence, as when someone has a medical problem which many know yet none can mention to the patient because it is private, even when the patient wants to talk about it but doesn't for fear he will invade the private feelings of the others. It's used promotionally, as in invitations from menswear shops to "our semi-annual private sale—save 20 to 75%."

Because the word "privacy" is used so widely and so loosely, the concept remains inexact. No doubt, language will evolve to meet the challenge. Makeshift terms will be useful in the interim, for example: "access-control privacy," for matters of access to a person; "room-to-grow privacy," for matters of psychological, moral, or educational growth; "safety-valve privacy," for matters of temporarily shedding uncomfortable roles; "respect privacy," for matters of dignity versus debasement.

Another obstacle to discussions of privacy is doubt that privacy has value. The United States, even though it is at the leading edge of privacy protection, belongs to an active, congregational tradition. The term "privacy" implies withdrawal, and any suggestion that withdrawal has intrinsic value falls on deaf ears in this tradition. Withdrawal may have had value in itself in other parts of the world at other times, but in America the value of a withdrawal is measured by the usefulness of the return. As a result, many Americans resist the idea that privacy has intrinsic value. They are more open to the idea that it has instrumental value but remain uncertain about why this is so—even as they demand it.

Privacy, then, is a right whose time has come. It has always been essential to people's well-being; but as of the late twentieth century—like free speech in the mid-eighteenth century—it has not yet been fully established as a value.

NOTES

1. See Ruth Gavison, "Privacy and the Limits of Law," *Yale Law Journal* 89 (1980); 421.

2. Samuel D. Warren and Louis D. Brandeis, "The Right to Privacy," *Harvard Law Review* 4 (1890); 193.

3. Edward Shils, *Center and Periphery: Essays in Macrosociology* (Chicago: University of Chicago Press, 1975), pp. 320–329.

4. See Arnold J. Toynbee, *A Study of History* (New York: Oxford University Press, 1963), volumes 7, 8, and 9.

5. Glenn Negley, "Philosophical Views on the Value of Privacy." *Law and Contemporary Problems* 1, no. 2 (Spring 1966); 320.

6. For physical trespass, see *Dietemann v. Time*, 449 F.2d 245 (9th Cir. 1971); for public disclosure and for reckless falsehoods, see *Dresbach v. Doubleday*, 518 F.Supp. 1285 (DCDC 1981); for commercial exploitation, see *Zacchini v. Scripps-Howard*, 433 U.S. 562 (1977); for constitutional privacy, see *Griswold v. Connecticut*, 381 U.S. 479 (1965).

_____ Chapter 2 _____

Background: Through the American Golden Age of Privacy

As a factor in human life, privacy has long been present, even though, in Glenn Negley's words, it has been "casually presumed" and, as a question, "has been lurking at the fringes . . . awaiting consideration."[1] Anthropological and historical evidence indicates that most people have insisted upon having privacy, even though societies have differed dramatically in their emphases on it. The evidence is sufficient to indicate that a demand for various kinds of privacy and an intuitive understanding of them are built into human beings.

Unfortunately, anthropologists have given privacy little attention. Like others, they have casually presumed privacy existed without focusing on it. The result is that anyone seeking anthropological material on privacy must extract it from writings not indexed for privacy or intended as discussions about privacy, and otherwise rely on a small number of studies in which anthropologists have targeted the subject.

In 1971, John M. Roberts and Thomas Gregor described the economic and customary features that seemed to predispose a society to protecting types of privacy.[2] Roberts and Gregor defined privacy as domestic privacy and measured it in terms of the permeability of dwellings to sight and sound, the presence or absence of closable doors and windows, the presence or absence of partitions inside dwellings, and the number of persons who commonly lived together.[3] They confined themselves to relatively simple societies—those with low levels of political integration—because, the authors said, those with high political integration uniformly have had high levels of domestic privacy.[4]

They found that societies with domesticated plants and animals had higher levels of domestic privacy than those dependent on hunting, fishing, or gathering. High privacy was most strongly related to animal husbandry, particularly of large animals. High privacy was found in peoples who raised cattle. High privacy was also strongly associated with cereal crops. They also found privacy was higher where the gods were understood to be present, active, and supportive of human morality.[5] Roberts and Gregor also noted that more games of strategy were played where privacy was high. They suggested that privacy may have been a Neolithic development. They also suggested that human surveillance decreases when it is replaced by the surveillance of a high god.[6]

Their citing of the Neolithic, the period that witnessed the birth of agriculture, as a starting point for privacy contrasts with studies of fishing and hunting societies that survived into modern times in which people also found room to incorporate privacy into their lives. If these surviving hunters made room for privacy, most likely so did earlier participants in an upper Paleolithic economy. This would date privacy from 35,000 years ago, when modern people in hunting societies first appeared in the caves of what became Europe,[7] or earlier. Those who believe that the Neanderthalers were another modern people who bred into the lines extant today date privacy back an additional 75,000 years to the time when Neanderthal hunting society became evident in the archeological record.[8]

Even if privacy has been with us only from the start of the Neolithic, about 9,000 years ago, it has been with us a long time. However, animal studies indicate that many creatures require what we would call privacy.[9] As a result, it would not be surprising to discover that a need for and an understanding of types of privacy has been with us from our beginnings.

According to Barrington Moore, Eskimos and Pygmies—now usually identified by the tribal names Inuit and BaMbuti—two successful hunter-gatherer groups that retained the upper Paleolithic economy into the twentieth century, develop close and dependent relationships in their communities. In both groups, however, said Moore, emotional reticence is used to preserve a sense of privacy.[10] Among both, individuals have traditionally forced themselves to be cordial and have suppressed resentments. A similar mechanism is employed by civilized people living in conditions of high density. A recent study in Hong Kong found that people there frequently restrict emotional involvement with others as a privacy-enhancing strategy.[11]

Generally, said Moore, privacy is minimal where technology and social organization are also minimal. "Privacy," he said, "cannot be the dominant value in any society."[12] It is, he said, an evolutionary product of social development. It exists in primitive societies as a desire to sometimes escape from others, but it became a more important conscious need as public authority grew.[13]

In traditional Inuit dwellings, each person had a spot on the floor along a wall and had an option to participate in the talk or not. Moore described men who occasionally faced toward a wall and remained so for most of a day; they were not addressed by others, despite heavy activity in the dwelling.[14] For these descriptions of the pre-modern life of the Inuit, Moore relied upon a study by Jean L. Briggs.

Reporting on her years with natives of the Canadian North, Briggs described her own experience with privacy in Inuit dwellings. Moving into a winter house with a family, after living her first months alone in her own tent, loomed as a crisis for Briggs. She wrote that she dreaded the lack of privacy that would be the result of moving into a ten-foot room with two children under the age of seven plus three other members of a family. She discovered, however, that her fears were groundless. "But on the whole," she wrote, "to my surprise, the human warmth and peacefulness of the household, and the uncanny sensitivity of its members to unspoken wishes, created an atmosphere in which the privacy of my tent came to seem in memory a barren thing."[15]

In the sleeping and living area of the dwelling, she was given a spot on the floor. She wrote:

> That spot, just the length and breadth of my sleeping bag, very quickly became my spot, and from it I always looked out on the same view. The sameness of it gave me a sense of stability in a world of shifting dwellings, a feeling of belonging in a family; it even gave me a sense of privacy, since no one ever encroached on my space without permission, and sitting there I could withdraw quietly from conversation into an inner world, reading or writing, or observing the doings of the rest of the family and their friends without disturbance.[16]

Other peoples living until recently outside complex societies have managed to build privacy into their habits. The Siriono, a central Amazonian tribe, Moore wrote, confined bodily functions to secluded forest locations, except at night.[17] In seeking seclusion for bodily functions, the Siriono, said Moore, were behaving as have most peoples studied by anthropologists. Most excluded all but intimate others from occasions of defecation, urination, or sexual intercourse. In fact, Moore suggested, a sense of disgust at witnessing such events is a learned response that protects against intrusion. An interesting variation, Moore noted, was in the traditional standards of the Fulani, of the African Sahel, who could show no bodily needs or urges in public and could not even eat with some people, but who were free to urinate in public.[18]

A well-known people in anthropological literature who regulate privacy in a striking manner are the Tuaregs, pastoralists of the central Sahara. Tuareg men go veiled, and, according to Robert M. Murphy, writing in 1964, manipulate their veils to regulate social distance.[19] These veils cover the lower part of the face, but can be pulled higher to conceal all but eye slots. Tuareg men, Murphy reported, constantly re-adjust their veils, in effect reeling in and out social distance moment by moment, and reducing their faces to eye slots when they are on delicate social ground. They do not remove their veils even when they are eating.

Village life in complex societies may be organized to protect privacy. Jeffrey S. Victor reported in 1980 that in Orival, France, most homes were surrounded by walls or fences.[20] Gates giving entrance within the walls were often locked, and frequently bore the warning "dangerous dog." German shepherds or Dobermans could be seen in some yards. Most residents would refuse entry by simply not going to the gate, Victor said. Many used misinformation to control visiting—for example, by giving false information of a time when a visitor might expect to find someone at home. Also, they would use unfriendliness, said Victor. Co-workers at a local plant had little social contact after work. Half of the women had little contact with neighbors.

Similarly, residents of Zinacantan township in Chiapas, southern Mexico, as described by Leslie K. and John B. Haviland in 1983, were extremely privacy conscious.[21] Homesteads, the Havilands said, were characterized by "zones of admission." These were located in various areas: just outside the gate; in the patio; on the porch; inside the house in the visitors' area; and by the fire. Entry into each new stage was by invitation only.[22] These houses had no windows. Two men of the village shared food cooked over a single fire only if they worked together on a single patch of land to grow it. The villagers avoided extended family living arrangements. Marriages sometimes failed because of the stress caused by the new wife's living for a time in the husband's home of origin, from which she became a channel to outsiders of information about the family. The Havilands described village women pulling up scarves to cover their faces as they waited in line at a mill to have their corn ground. The authors noted as a paradox that in this privacy-conscious community one felt oppressed by prying eyes.[23]

All human societies have in common the incest taboo—broken surprisingly often, it appears, in twentieth-century America.[24] Only a few societies have endorsed incest within the nuclear family and those have done so only under very special circumstances—brother-sister marriage, for example, in the ruling families of ancient Egypt.[25]

The incest taboo has been viewed as mainly a privacy protection device by one writer, Yehudi A. Cohen. If he is right, the concern for privacy has been as widespread as the incest taboo; in other words, present in all societies from the most primitive to the most advanced; and, because the most primitive differ little from the prehistorical, probably in all societies that have ever existed.

The need to be free of extreme emotional and physical stimulation, especially from other people, underlies the incest taboo, according to Cohen, writing in 1964. This need, Cohen said, varies in strength as it is unfulfilled or satisfied, and its strength and importance to the person varies among individuals.[26] The need, said Cohen, is stronger during certain developmental spurts and is particularly strong during the ages three to five and during early and late puberty.

"The need for privacy is one of the motive forces in the individual's orientation to the world around him. . . . [O]ne of the functions of the ego is to control as needed the volume and intensity of stimulation from other people," he wrote.[27] Children, he said, must develop a certainty that they can gratify their need for privacy. However, they cannot develop it if they are subjected to sexual experiences before developing "the degree of maturity called ego strength." In addition, Cohen wrote, sexual experiences within the family are more intense because of the close involvement of family members with one another; therefore, in the family, the child must be doubly protected.[28] In Cohen's view, failure to provide such protection produces schizophrenics, immature persons, and persons without enough sense of separateness to function as individuals in carrying out tasks different from those of others.[29] Cohen's argument is convincing enough to indicate that the incest taboo might be taken as anthropological proof that some sensitivity to privacy has been common to all people since the beginning of the first societies.

The desire for privacy among the young apparently is constant enough so that far less serious offenses than incest can thwart it. In a 1981 study, American teenagers cited privacy as a high priority for them. Children with brothers and sisters listed lack of privacy as their chief complaint. The authors of the study offered parents advice based upon children's indications of their need for privacy. The advice included: Don't walk into rooms without knocking, listen to phone conversations, read diaries or mail, expect children to tell everything, throw away or give away items without asking, or go through desks or dressers; do control invasions of privacy by siblings.[30]

Just as signs of privacy can be found in anthropologically studied societies, they can also be found in historical societies, those which have left their own records. Through some of the historical societies there runs a wariness of privacy.

In Athens in the fourth century B.C., for example, according to Moore, privacy had a clear place—it characterized the home life.[31] The polis, the political realm, stayed out of marriages, except to care for orphans, pregnant widows, or families facing extinction. Sex generally was regarded as a private matter. A husband's taking of whatever revenge he preferred in response to adultery was a private matter.[32] Publicly endorsed rules restricted the access of lower strata males to women of higher strata. However, Athenians were biased against the private, which carried for them a connotation of being common or vulgar.[33]

Moore found hostility to privacy in Plato.[34] The Athenian society, Moore asserted, was based on the creation of a public realm because it was a warrior society supported by taxes.[35] The Athenians—like the journalists who in 1988 exposed Senator Gary Hart's peccadillo—believed that private morality was relevant to judging probable political performance.[36]

In the view of Hannah Arendt, the Greeks disliked privacy because it was the realm of animal necessity but was not uniquely human.[37] Privacy referred to the household, which was the zone of family hierarchy and economic necessity. It was a life from which Greek men fled to a second life of political participation, the polis life of equality and freedom.[38] The Greek concept of public and private was very different from the modern conception, Arendt asserted. What moderns call public is in large degree the household realm of the Greeks expanded to a national or international scale—in effect, matters of economic necessity gone public. What moderns call private, the protection of the intimate, developed, Arendt asserted, in reaction to the expanded household realm—the social realm—not in reaction to the polis.[39] To extrapolate, the intimate side of the private life was, in classical Greece, hidden in a household realm that itself was not public and therefore could be taken for granted, even disdained; there was no threat to it.

In Moore's view, Old Testament Hebrew society made less room for the private than did Greece.[40] This was a religious community, not a political one; there was no polis. The community ran on moral obligations, and these did not stop at the front door of the house.[41] The Tenth Commandment of the Bible, Moore asserted, introduced public morality into what would have been a private zone in Athens.[42] There was no privacy from Yahweh; every secret thing came to judgment.[43] Religious rules were imposed on the conduct of daily life.[44] The obligations to care for the poor and unfortunate fell not on the polis but on the individual.[45] Nevertheless, Moore asserted, the Hebrews did respect privacy, as indicated by limitations placed on the kings and the rules against nakedness.[46]

A third historical society examined by Moore was China from the sixth to third centuries B.C. A distinction between public and private had been made in China prior to this period, said Moore. Taoism already existed as a pro-privacy philosophy. But life in China was meticulously organized under rules of etiquette. These rules allowed some room for privacy, but private expression was regarded as a threat or an affront to the smooth functioning of the community.[47]

According to Moore, ancient Athens and China recognized public and private realms. Both, along with the Hebrews, protected individual rights. But privacy had an antisocial connotation in all three. Moore asserted that although privacy cannot be the dominant value in any society, the desire for some privacy is a universal trait.[48]

Some later historical steps in the development of privacy, Moore wrote, were the articulation of the Protestant Christian standard of private-personal contact with the deity, and the rise of the professions and of scholarship under the bourgeoisie—study being a socially constructive use of privacy.

In Europe and America, privacy was largely taken for granted prior to the nineteenth century. Practices in some locations in early America clearly were discouraging to persons seeking privacy. The Massachusetts Bay Colony provides an example of an anti-privacy posture, with its tithingmen, each charged with surveilling ten families, and with a public confession being required before full church membership could be offered.[49] Some of the American utopian communities also provided little privacy.[50] But America did provide much open space, so much that in the westward migrations, loneliness was probably a greater problem than privacy. American families, according to Philip Blumstein and Pepper Schwartz, have always guarded their privacy. The American family, they have written, always was a small unit. Even in the eighteenth century, a family was often only husband, wife, and three children. There has never been a strong tradition of the extended family, they said, and little expectation of the extended family living under one roof.[51]

In England, according to several views, privacy has been protected for many centuries—and continues to be protected despite the absence of any English law of privacy. English protections often cited are the common law rules ostensibly aimed at other problems but secondarily protecting privacies. These included common law prohibitions of trespass, burglary, eavesdropping, voyeurism, libel, and slander; plus the common law principle that a man's home was his castle.[52] These common law principles were imported into American law and offered indirect protection in the United States also.

According to Alan F. Westin, privacy has been less threatened in Britain than in the United States or Germany because in Britain it was built into a tradition of tolerance for nonconformity, reserve and deference.[53] Edward T. Hall also has noted that the English have built greater respect for privacy into individual manners than have Americans or Germans. The English, Hall observed, do not close doors as a way to get privacy but instead just close off contact with others present.

Other English people will respect this, said Hall, whereas Americans may refuse to stop talking to the person who wants the privacy. Also, said Hall, the English simply speak more quietly.[54] Walter F. Pratt has suggested that the English are so oriented to privacy, and go so far in guarding their own and respecting that of others, that little protection has been required from governmental institutions.[55] Herbert J. Spiro has tried to explain the English tradition of respecting privacy as a result of the development of English law. The separation of law from the rest of government, he suggested, frustrated the establishment of investigative and intrusive powers in the government, while the common law procedures were used as models for other relationships, in particular the strategy of disclosing only what is needed to win a point.[56] In sum, it is agreed upon by several observers that the English have developed traditions of respecting privacy and that the content and manner of the common law contributed to this development.

The same observers suggest that the continental European experience with privacy has been different. According to Spiro, intrusions on privacy by European governments were so extensive that people learned to take a posture of resistance to the intrusions and to compensate for losses of privacy to government by protecting privacy against intrusion by other people.[57] Germans, according to Hall, are very sensitive to private space and use architectural devices to protect it. They traditionally have used heavy doors, and they keep them closed, he said.[58] According to Westin, the threat to privacy in Germany is in an authoritarian tendency that makes the privacy of the critic and non-conformist insecure, whereas in the United States the threat is in egalitarian tendencies, including a "leveling curiosity" and pressure to conform to middle-class standards.[59] Westin found privacy to be less threatened in Britain.[60] Spiro suggested in 1971 that Americans sought less privacy than continental Europeans and English, hesitating to share private information with governments but sharing it eagerly with others in society.[61]

One can easily overlook or undervalue the advent of the professions and the need for study as key events in the growth of respect for privacy. All societies that require for their continuation the growth of knowledge and its professional application must train people to accept periods of isolation in which to work with their own thoughts, and they must encourage others to respect this quiet study time. No matter how totalitarian a society's leaders seek to be, if the continuation of the society is based at all on study, they will have to provide some privacy to some of their people. As a result, the advent of the professions, schools, and formalized education made a degree of privacy a noticeable instrumental necessity. As the professions spread from their beginnings in Europe in the late Middle Ages, they made one element of privacy—room for solitary effort—a requirement almost everywhere. Of course, scholarly traditions among elites existed in East Asia, the Middle East, India, and elsewhere, and also in Europe, prior to the late European Middle Ages.

The spread of books, starting in the century following the invention of the printing press, encouraged privacy. According to George Steiner,

> The practice of reading a book to oneself, in silence, is a specific, late historical development. It implies a number of economic and social pre-conditions: a room of one's own . . . or, at least, a home spacious enough to allow areas of quiet; the private possession of books . . . , means of artificial light during evening hours. . . . The man who reads alone in a room with his mouth closed, from a volume which he owns, is a special product of Western bourgeois literacy and leisure.[62]

Edward Shils has suggested that the nineteenth century was a golden age of privacy in Western societies. During that century, he said, industrial growth produced enough wealth to support private living arrangements, except among the poor; and urbanization had broken up village communities; yet social science research had not advanced, nor had the technology of surveillance.[63] This nineteenth-century privacy was a pleasant result of custom and circumstance. It received no direct legal protection, nor any attention in philosophical discourse. The great liberal Western philosophers were silent about privacy: Kant, Locke, Mill, Rousseau.[64]

Changes in home life may have contributed to the growth of privacy in nineteenth-century America. According to Maxine Van de Wetering, the eighteenth-century American home was tied to outside society and served it, but the nineteenth-century home was separated from the outside and served as an alternative to the values of the industrial revolution. The nineteenth-century home was valued for its privacy, she said, and houses were designed to satisfy the wish to be alone.[65] The nineteenth-century home, she said, "was a primary place to gain the kind of nurture that resulted in self-knowledge, self-realization, and even self-redemption."[66] She suggested that religious crises in the early part of the century had weakened the church as an institution for providing basic trust, coherence, and stability, and that some people had begun to seek the same at home.[67]

Moore too suggested that the nineteenth century was special in the history of privacy, but Moore focused his attention on England. He suggested that Victorian England provided more political freedom and privacy than any society before it, and that the control of instincts was a part of the Victorian formula.[68]

Moore also noted that a key step in the growth of privacy as a value was the idea that the individual, not the group or estate, was the basic unit of society.[69] Factors contributing to this idea, he suggested, were the industrial revolution, the success of the bourgeoisie, and the rise of the professions.[70] All three matured as trends in the nineteenth century. At the end of the nineteenth century, Moore said, the benefits of privacy flowed mainly to "propertied and employing" classes, but others wanted some of these benefits.[71]

Other signs that the nineteenth century was important in the development of privacy can be found in the works of Henry James. One story in particular that explored a theme of privacy was *The Private Life*,[72] in which James portrayed one character who was entirely public, ceasing to function—or to exist—when alone, but functioning brilliantly in public, and another character who was entirely private—a writer—who was represented in public by a double, the shallow character who ceased to function when alone. The dominating figure of the story was the entirely private writer, whom the reader never meets. The entirely public man was, at his best, merely charming and tactful. The entirely private one, however, turned out to have the stature of greatness. James seemed to have been voting for privacy and for the private.

Conditions, then, at the close of the nineteenth century were right for an advance in the awareness of privacy and in concern for its protection. Many people outside the lower classes had grown accustomed to a high level of privacy—in anthropological terms, to having their in-born desire for privacy satisfied in large measure—even though, in Richard Hixson's view, privacy had never taken more than second place behind other needs, such as defense, collective survival, or sociability.[73] In addition, industrial societies had risen well above the subsistence line, and industrial wealth could support private houses with individual rooms even for those of moderate means and for those who had to rent. Also, cities, with their offer of anonymity, had grown. And all of this was taking place in relatively cold climates, which, Shils suggested, encouraged privacy, presumably by demanding heavy clothing and dwellings complex enough to provide by conscious architectural design some of the privacy available out-of-doors in warm climates year-round.[74]

At the close of the nineteenth century, intrusions into the previously available privacy began to accumulate. Steps to give privacy explicit legal protection got under way in the United States and France,[75] as intrusions into the previously taken-for-granted privacy advanced.

The main intruders of the first decades of the twentieth century, said Shils, were private investigators working for private corporations in the United States, journalists of the popular press, personnel recruiters for large corporations, and psychological researchers.[76] Since World War II, said Shils, the main invaders have been social science researchers (particularly because they switched their method from participant observation to sample surveys), employees of government agencies, advanced surveillance personnel, business security specialists, communications technologists, consumer credit lenders, and advertisers.[77]

Reviewing from England the constriction of previously assumed types of privacy, H. J. McCloskey listed what he considered to be widely accepted inroads into privacy:

> [I]ntelligence and other psychological and medical tests for their children, where information obtained may be stored in data banks; . . . questionnaires by schools, universities, employers, banks, creditors. . . . They demand that their newspapers report news based on invasions of privacy of those in the public eye, those before the courts, and those who suffer great misfortune or good fortune, and they seek to foster in those whose privacy is invaded the belief that they ought to consent to such invasions of their privacy.[78]

According to Vance Packard, the popularity of whose 1964 book *The Naked Society* might itself be considered a historical marker of an increased constituency for the protection of privacy, five forces undermined privacy in the twentieth century:

1. An increase in "organized living," bringing growth of private and governmental organizations needing to control their members as a feature of size, and also bringing invasive police measures to control urban crime;

2. Movement to garrison state mentality at mid-century with corporations and government agencies following a tight security model even when not handling classified material;

3. Pressure generated by abundance, including proprietary secrecy by companies competing in vogue-ridden markets, market surveys, and an appetite for the entertainments provided by the mass media's privacy invasions;

4. Growth of investigation as a private industry; and,

5. Advances in electronic equipment.[79]

Observers, then, have noted that a crop of ways to invade privacy sprang up in the twentieth century. Some of these clearly had nineteenth-century roots. The Pinkertons flourished in the late nineteenth century, and governmental bureaucratic complexity began to grow. Proprietary secrecy is at least as old as the Coca-Cola Company, founded in 1892; and it was invasions of privacy by newspaper reporters that inspired the 1890 law review article that started American privacy law.[80] However, the accumulation of intrusions in the twentieth century is remarkable for anyone who has eyes to see it, and contrasts dramatically with the nineteenth-century golden age as described by Shils.

Some commentators on the most recent history of privacy—that since 1960—have stressed that relationships of individuals to formal organizations have changed. Shils has noted that privacy has become an increasing problem because it has been swamped "in the expansion of the powers and ambitions of elites and in the difficulties that they encounter in attempting to govern and protect and please vast collectivities."[81]

A more detailed presentation of a similar idea was offered by James Rule, Douglas McAdam, Linda Stearns, and David Uglow in 1980. New demands for information arose in the 1960s and 1970s as part of new relationships of individuals to formal organizations, they argued.[82] The development of these new demands, they said, was independent of the spread of computers and other electronic aids to information gathering and storage.[83] The need for detailed personal records arises from complex obligations and "extended mutual dependency" between organizations and their publics, they asserted.[84] They listed labor unions; the Internal Revenue Service and other governmental agencies; agencies of registration of births, deaths, marriages, and passports; professional organizations; business corporations; and educational systems. These organizations, they said, cannot function without information on people.[85] A relaxation of data collection would reduce organizational efficiency, but, they argued, adequate efficiency would remain, and privacy would be enhanced.[86]

Another explanation for the increase in concern for privacy is simply that the growth in the possibilities of enjoying much privacy in affluent settings now coexists with the development of highly effective means to invade it.[87] Some recent studies in the United States, United Kingdom, and Canada indicate that people in these countries are increasingly concerned about their privacy and possibly are growing reluctant to disclose information about themselves. Goyder and Leiper set out to discover why response rates in interview surveys of general populations have declined since the end of the 1960s—by 20 percent, according to some reports.[88] The authors developed a "privacy index," based on newspaper reports articulating privacy-related objections to censuses as a percentage of all newspaper reports on censuses. They included American, British, and Canadian newspapers. In 1985 they reported that their privacy index increased during the same period in which survey responses declined—since 1960.[89] The authors did not insist that privacy concerns were the sole reasons for the decline in survey responses but suggested that they were one factor.[90] The U.S. Census Bureau, it might be noted, had unexpected difficulty in getting participation in its 1990 census.

Also in 1985, Vidmar and Flaherty reported that many survey respondents in Ontario believed that organizations collect more information than they need. A large portion of persons surveyed—68 percent—said they had less personal privacy than ten years earlier. The authors suggested that concern for privacy was a latent political issue that could emerge if particular incidents provoke it.[91]

Privacy, then, has always been important and to some degree available, but beginning in Western countries in the nineteenth century people began to consciously enjoy it. Then, in these same countries in the twentieth century, people began to notice that they had lost some of the privacy they thought they had. The twentieth century was a technological century—a high-tech era, in its second half; as a result, it is tempting to attribute the loss of privacy to technology. Not all commentators have done this, however.

For example, August Heckscher wrote in the late 1950s regarding privacy that "decay of the inner life precedes the invasion from the outside—as usually happens when the overthrow of states is involved."[92] As a result, Heckscher challenged the view that technological changes have caused what he considered to be an erosion of the foundation of privacy.[93] Borrowing from Arendt, he said that the Greeks had robbed private life of vitality to feed the public life, the Middle Ages had robbed secular life to feed the sacred, and the modern West was robbing both public and private life of vitality to feed the social life, which he defined as the realm of "necessary unity and practical compromises."[94] He contended that when the social becomes dominant, "life lacks both inward depth and external adventure."[95]

Following Heckscher's example, one might look beyond technological explanations for some idea of what the privacy concept may be up against, and in the service of which technology is being employed. Probably, this is the idea that most human interactions and communications should be personalized.

Christopher Clausen, writing in 1985 had a sense for what may be at stake.[96] Personalization, he wrote, produced "counterfeits of intimacy in public situations, the synthetic emotions of the TV game show, a decline in respect for privacy, a literature that has become predominantly confessional (some would say exhibitionistic) and autobiographical, an electorate that votes for or against politicians largely on the basis of their personalities as communicated by television."[97]

He wrote:

> The effects of compulsive informality in public life and discourse are fairly evident. Its effect on private life is no less dreary. The rituals of courtship, of the making of friends, of growing old are all in serious disrepair, so much so that one can hardly discuss them without seeming nostalgic. But let's say it anyway: one of the best arguments against having sex on the first date is that it leaves nowhere else to go, thereby short-circuiting the

whole process of rituals by which true intimacy and knowledge of another person have to be created. There is a pace at which formality and reserve yield naturally to intimacy; when that pace is forced, the relationship is likely to remain permanently superficial. . . . [98]

When everyone is a first name and intimacy is the sought-for ideal in all situations, both intimacy and judgment become harder to reach than ever; hypocrisy or disappointment inevitably takes their place most of the time.[99]

As a result, he reported, when a new dental receptionist asked him, "Are you Chris?" he replied, "I'm Mr. Clausen."[100] Perhaps he went too far in his response to the receptionist, but he did have an impressive grasp of the problem.

Against the anthropological and historical background, the explicit concern for privacy evident in the late twentieth century is not surprising. People universally need some privacy. Although most have taken the satisfaction of this need for granted, many in Western societies have in recent centuries enjoyed considerable satisfaction of this need. But much has happened during this century to reduce the level of enjoyment. This abrupt change has been great enough to shift privacy in many minds from the category of "assumed and taken for granted" to the category of "threatened—explicit protection required." The fact that the concern for privacy stems in part paradoxically from our own forfeiting of privacy to achieve goals of personal safety, affluence, greater satisfaction of wants, social security, full discharge of obligations by institutions, and comprehensive news reporting has not diminished the intensity of the concern.

NOTES

1. Glenn Negley, "Philosophical Views on the Value of Privacy," *Law and Contemporary Problems* 1, no. 2 (Spring 1966); 320.
2. John M. Roberts and Thomas Gregor, "Privacy: A Cultural

View," in J. Roland Pennock and John W. Chapman, *Privacy*, (New York: Atherton, 1971).

3. Ibid., 202.

4. Ibid.

5. If alternative types of gods do not immediately come to mind, consider a distant but vengeful one, an amoral one, a mere prime mover.

6. Roberts and Gregor, "Privacy" in Pennock and Chapman, *Privacy*, p. 202.

7. Richard E. Leakey, *The Making of Mankind* (New York: Dutton, 1981).

8. Ibid.

9. Yehudi A. Cohen, *The Transition From Childhood to Adolescence* (Chicago: Aldine, 1964), p. 163.

10. Barrington Moore, Jr., *Privacy*, (Armonk, NY: M.E. Sharpe, 1984).

11. Harold Travers, "Orientation Toward Privacy in Hong Kong," *Perceptual and Motor Skills* 59 (1984); 635–644.

12. Moore, *Privacy*, p. 20.

13. Ibid., p. 17.

14. Ibid., pp. 3–23.

15. Jean L. Briggs, *Never in Anger* (Cambridge: Harvard University Press, 1970), p. 79.

16. Ibid., p. 77.

17. Because they feared the night forest, he said, they produced piles of feces outside their dwellings.

18. Moore, *Privacy*, pp. 59–71.

19. Robert M. Murphy, "Social Distance and the Veil," *American Anthropologist* 66 (1964); 1257–1274.

20. Jeffrey S. Victor, "Privacy, Intimacy and Shame in a French Village," in Stanton K. Tefft, ed., *Secrecy: A Cross-Cultural Perspective* (New York: Human Science Press, 1980).

21. Leslie K. Haviland and John B. Haviland, "Privacy in a Mexican Indian Village," in S. I. Benn and G. F. Gaus, eds., *Public and Private in Social Life* (New York: St. Martin's Press, 1983).

22. Ibid., p. 348.

23. Ibid., pp. 351–360.

24. Judith Lewis Herman, *Father-Daughter Incest* (Cambridge: Harvard University Press, 1980), pp. 7–21.

25. *Encyclopaedia Britannica*, 15th ed., 1985, vol. 19, Macropaedia, p. 62.

26. Cohen, *The Transition*, p. 161.

27. Ibid., p. 167.

28. Ibid., pp. 170–175.

29. Ibid., p. 168.

30. Jane Norman and Myron W. Harms, *The Private Life of the American Teenager* (New York: Rawson, Wade, 1981), p. 30.

31. Moore, *Privacy*, pp. 81–86.

32. Ibid., pp. 147–148.

33. Ibid., p. 83.

34. Ibid., p. 124.

35. Ibid., p. 109.

36. Ibid., p. 156.

37. Hannah Arendt, *The Human Condition* (Chicago: University of Chicago Press, 1958), p. 46.

38. Ibid., pp. 22–30.

39. Ibid., p. 49.

40. Moore, *Privacy*, pp. 168–210.

41. Ibid., p. 196.

42. Ibid., p. 190.

43. Ibid., pp. 172–173.

44. Ibid., p. 190.

45. Ibid., p. 196.

46. Ibid., pp. 179–181.

47. Ibid., pp. 219–266.

48. Ibid., p. 274 and p. 276.

49. See David Flaherty, *Privacy in Colonial New England* (Charlottesville: University of Virginia Press, 1972).

50. See John M. Whitworth, *God's Blueprints: A Sociological Study of Three Utopian Sects*. (Boston: Routledge and K. Paul, 1975).

51. Philip Blumstein and Pepper Schwartz, *American Couples* (New York: Morrow, 1983), p. 83.

52. See Ruth Gavison, "Privacy and the Limits of Law," *Yale Law Journal* 89 (1980); 464.

53. Alan F. Westin, *Privacy and Freedom* (New York: Atheneum, 1967), p. 26.

54. Edward T. Hall, *The Hidden Dimension* (New York: Doubleday, 1966), pp. 129–134.

55. Walter F. Pratt, *Privacy in Britain* (Lewisburg: Bucknell University Press, 1979), p. 16.

56. Herbert J. Spiro, "Privacy in Contemporary Perspective," in J. Roland Pennock and John W. Chapman, *Privacy* (New York: Atherton, 1971), pp. 121–140.

Judges in the European civil law system that was derived from Roman code law were civil servants with investigatory duties, who answered to the legislature or executive branches, whereas common law judges were essentially referees and belonged to a branch distinct from the rest of government.

57. Ibid.

58. Hall, *Hidden Dimension*, pp. 123–129.

59. Westin, *Privacy and Freedom*, pp. 27–28.

60. Ibid., p. 26.

61. Spiro, "Privacy," in Pennock and Chapman, *Privacy*.

62. George Steiner, "Literature and Post-History," in George Steiner, *Language and Silence* (New York: Atheneum, 1967), p. 383.

63. Edward Shils, *Center and Periphery: Essays in Macrosociology* (Chicago: University of Chicago Press, 1975), p. 323.

64. H. J. McCloskey, "Privacy and the Right to Privacy," *Philosophy* 55 (1980); 17–18.

65. Maxine Van de Wetering, "The Popular Concept of 'Home' in Nineteenth-Century America," *Journal of American Studies* 18, no. 1 (1984); 5–28.

66. Ibid., p. 25.

67. Ibid., pp. 5–14.

68. Barrington Moore, Jr., "Privacy," *Society* 22, no. 4 (May/June 1985); 17–27.

69. Ibid., p. 25.

70. Ibid.

71. Ibid.

72. Henry James, "The Private Life," *The Novels and Tales of Henry James*, New York Edition, Vol. 17 (New York: Kelley, 1970). See also Henry James, "The Reverberator," *The Novels and Tales of Henry James*, New York Edition, Vol. 13 (New York: Kelley, 1970).

73. Richard F. Hixson, *Privacy in a Public Society* (New York: Oxford University Press, 1967), p. 8.

74. Shils, *Center and Periphery*, p. 323.

75. Samuel D. Warren and Louis D. Brandeis, "The Right to Privacy," *Harvard Law Review* 4 (1890); 193.

76. Shils, *Center and Periphery*, p. 323.

77. Ibid.

78. H. J. McCloskey, "Privacy and the Right to Privacy," *Philosophy* 55 (1980); 23.

79. Vance Packard, *The Naked Society* (New York: D. McKay, 1964), pp. 15–43.

80. Warren and Brandeis, "Privacy," p. 193.

81. Edward Shils, "Privacy: Its Constitution and Vicissitudes," *Law and Contemporary Problems* 1, no. 2 (Spring 1966); p. 305.

82. James Rule et al., *The Politics of Privacy* (New York: Elsevier, 1980).

83. Ibid., p. 12.

84. Ibid., p. 46.

85. Ibid., p. 45.

86. Ibid., p. 164.

87. H. J. McCloskey, "Privacy and the Right to Privacy," p. 17. One explanation for why privacy has grown as a legal concept in the United States is that it has presented a strategic option for escaping the limitations of defamation as a legal concept, for basing personal rights on something other than the concept of property, and for avoiding the use of the term "substantive due process." Ruth Gavison, "Privacy and the Limits of Law," pp. 466–467.

88. John Goyder and Jean McKenzie Leiper, "The Decline in Survey Response: A Social Values Interpretation," *Sociology* 19, no. 1 (1985); 55.

89. Ibid., pp. 62–71.

90. Ibid.

91. Neil Vidmar and David H. Flaherty, "Concern for Personal Privacy in an Electronic Age," *Journal of Communications* 35, no. 2 (1985); 91–104.

92. August Heckscher, "The Invasion of Privacy (2)—The Reshaping of Privacy," *The American Scholar* 28, no. 1 (1959); 11–20.

93. Ibid.

94. Ibid., p. 29.

95. Ibid., p. 20.

96. Christopher Clausen, "A Decent Impersonality," *The American Scholar* 54, no. 4 (1985); 537–540.

97. Ibid., p. 538.

98. Ibid., p. 539.

99. Ibid., p. 540.

100. Ibid., p. 537.

_____ Chapter 3 _____

Background: Those Left Out of the Golden Age

The nineteenth-century golden age of privacy in Western societies generally,[1] as well as in the United States,[2] was not enjoyed by everyone. In the United States the largest groups left
out of the golden age were the black poor and the white poor.
Because almost all blacks were poor, this meant almost all
blacks. Not only did most blacks not enjoy the golden age, but
most were routinely subjected to invasions of privacy as a part
of slavery well into the second half of the century.

The increased conscious demand for privacy during the
twentieth century is traceable in part to the loss of this golden
age. By the end of the nineteenth century, the casually accepted
but broad privacy enjoyed during the period was swamped by
swelling industrial bureaucracies, increases in the scale of government, police methodology modeled on the Pinkertons, meddlesome newspaper reporters, and the arrival of social science
research. Calls for privacy protection started in the 1890s and
continued into the twentieth century as expanded military bureaucracies, the draft, the income tax, broadcast mass media,
electronic surveillance, computerization, national security jus-
tifications, and the social science and market-research ques-

tionnaire took hold. As most Americans were swept along from complacent enjoyment of privacy, to irritation at the increase of invasions, to insistence that privacy be explicitly protected—an insistence later satisfied to a degree by the privacy invasion torts,[3] the constitutional privacy right,[4] the Privacy Act,[5] the Fair Credit Reporting Act,[6] and other data-control legislation—the black poor and the white poor were left out of the process. Their descendants, however, are not uninterested in privacy. On the contrary, most are as demanding of privacy as other Americans. This fact indicates that the golden age cannot be the sole explanation for the concern for privacy generally evident in the late twentieth century.

BLACK AMERICANS

In the nineteenth century, as in the eighteenth and seventeenth centuries, invasions of privacy were used against blacks as instruments of control during slavery. After slavery was ended, the habit of invading the privacy of blacks continued in much of the country as a feature of the Jim Crow era, which lasted until about 1960. The severity and frequency of the invasions declined following emancipation. Yet slave era customs for controlling blacks persisted in the most segregated states, and these customs included insults to privacy. In addition, poverty reduced the availability of privacy to most blacks. Blacks experienced a particular lack of privacy because invasions of privacy were used against them as devices of control and domination.

Arguably, African customs did not provide much privacy to the ancestors of black Americans before American slavery was begun. By Western standards, traditional African societies often appear to be oppressively communal or authoritarian.[7] As a result, many blacks enslaved in the Americas must have arrived without much conscious orientation toward privacy. This, however, need not have been an obstacle to acquiring enthusiasm for it. Many urban as well as rural communities everywhere, including in Europe, were not respectful of privacy; so that if Africans were less privacy oriented than Europeans, it was only by degree.

An articulated ideal of individual rights and liberties was available to Europeans for over a thousand years because of the combination of the ancient Greek political model, the Christian concept of a personalizing God, and the Northern European custom of organizing power not hierarchically but by sharing it among peers led by the first among peers. In no other part of the world had individual rights been taken as seriously as they had been in Europe, even though the rights existed there more in theory than in reality until the seventeenth century. Even in the 1990s, most of the world's cultural and political traditions attributed greater value to the commonality's interests than to the individual's interests. Because privacy is an individual interest, in theory Europeans were closer to it than were Africans at the time American slavery started.

In practice, however, there may have been little difference. Probably, medieval life in Europe resembled life at the same time in the medieval African kingdoms, which then had not yet collapsed from internal breakdown or external pressures from Europe or the Middle East.

Also, Africa is an enormous continent; and, even in the late twentieth century, it was sparsely populated despite accelerated population growth in many African countries[8]—an acceleration halted in some countries toward the end of the century by acquired immune deficiency syndrome (AIDS). In pre-urbanization years, it must always have been possible to achieve a profound sense of privacy anywhere in Africa by simply walking away from a village.

The situation there resembled that in colonial America and on the frontiers of the newly formed United States. In colonial eastern America, people who wanted privacy could simply walk out into the woods; there was plenty of empty space; and a semblance of privacy could be maintained even in communities, like those of the Massachusetts Bay Colony, that endorsed surveillance.[9] Frontier America provided so much privacy that privacy was almost intolerable; settlers were spread out and isolated.

As a result, although the Africans enslaved in the United States may not have been privacy oriented, they probably were as familiar with privacy in practice as many of their white neighbors. The great obstacles to black Americans' experience of privacy were slavery, the systematic discrimination that followed emancipation and persisted for ten decades, and poverty, particularly urban poverty.

Unlike others from elsewhere in the world, who could adopt a trust in privacy as an individual right before or as soon as they arrived in North America, most blacks had the opposite experience: they learned in the middle passage, on slave auction platforms, and on farms and plantations that invasions of their privacy were what they could count on, that they would be afforded few privacies.

The invasion of privacy was at the core of the exploitation of blacks in America. What was ugliest about slavery was that slaves had to live stripped naked of privacy. Their houses, families, love relationships, and bodies were invaded without their being able to impose sure limits. Overseers or masters could enter their cabins at will. Families could be fractured by sale and shipment of family members, although some planters apparently tried to avoid this. Love relationships were broken the same way, and also by whites' taking of sexual favors with slave women, a common occurrence. Bodies were invaded by rape and physical punishments. The invasions were performed regularly enough to keep the spirits of slaves shattered and the dominance of whites clear.

Slavery in the Americas, after all, was not merely hard labor without pay required of persons otherwise protected by law. If it had been merely forced labor, it would not project the sickening ambiance that makes it appear, from the twentieth century, a disease rather than simply an exploitation of workers. To say that some black Americans remained angry into the late twentieth century simply because their ancestors were used as forced labor hardly captures the essence. A history of mere forced labor could not provoke real anger; if it could, the descendants of English and white American mill workers and child laborers would be seriously angry about the treatment visited on their ancestors before 1850. Whites and other nonblacks who mistakenly believe that slavery was merely forced labor can be excused for failing to understand why some blacks continued to be angry 130 years after emancipation.

On the other hand, to say that some blacks remained angry because their ancestors were subjected to invasions of privacy that struck them to the quick, humiliated them, sickened them, and successfully broke the spirit and rattled the brains of all too many nearly captures the essence. Asking these blacks to shake off the experience and to simply enjoy their late twentieth-century freedom without animosity is remarkably similar to asking a violently and sexually abused person to proceed without animosity toward the abusers, or asking a rape victim not to be angry at the rapist.

Slavery was a severe invasion of privacy. It struck to the quick. For many descendants of slaves, any reminder of it—even a small reminder—reinvoked the full-blown outrage. American racial practices through the 1960s contained regular, overt reminders. After the 1960s, reminders became more subtle; but some blacks, centuries of shabby treatment still vivid for them, were hyper-sensitive and super-vigilant. Outrage had been passed from generation to generation. It was still fresh in the 1990s. Without remembering that slavery was a system based on invading privacy, it was difficult to grasp the scope of the crime and therefore to understand why the outrage continued to surface.

Of course, slaves imported from Africa were not naive about slavery: Slavery was widespread in Africa. The prospects of many would have been no better had they been left in the African slave commerce rather than being sold into the American institution. Their privacy would have been invaded there, and their outrage would have been handed down against those of the tribal and nationality groups that perpetrated the slavery against them. One thinks of the continuing hostility between the Hutu and Tutsi in Rwanda and Burundi.

The transatlantic slave trade did not start because Europeans entered Africa with armies to capture people. It was not conducted by press gangs of Europeans scouring the continent with chains and muskets. It was simply a business arrangement between European ship captains and African entrepreneurs. Both thought they saw a big, new market opening up; they were right; both got rich. It was Africans who bought and caught slaves inland, applied the chains, marched the captives down to the coast, and sold slaves as cargo to Europeans.[10] If the American market had not been so large, the scope of the slavers' activities would have been more modest; and, in this way, whites can be held responsible for the damage done to Africa by the forced exportation of so many people.

However, for the whites involved the slave trade was a trade, not a military adventure. It became formally known as the Triangle Trade because the trading ships touched land at three points, making a profit at each point. They sold and offloaded slaves in the Caribbean or the American South, and there they bought sugar, molasses, rum, or other agricultural goods. They sailed to New England or England, where they sold the agricultural goods and bought manufactured goods, including textiles, weapons, tools, liquors, and money in the form of coins and articles of precious metals. Then they sailed to Africa where they used the manufactured goods to buy slaves. Even the Europeans who set up shop along the African coast as slave dealers did not make their living by leading expeditions to capture people. They were brokers. They bought slaves delivered to them. The enslaving process that sent millions of people to the Americas was an African business that had found a menacingly large market.

Almost all black Americans in the late twentieth century excused contemporary Africans for the complicity of earlier Africans in the slave trade. By contrast, a great many held contemporary white Americans accountable for the slaving activities of earlier whites. There are messages in this contrast: One is about geographical distance; another is about black Americans' struggles for a comfortable identity; but the third is about the invasion of privacy.

It is understandable that nearby perpetrators would be blamed more than far-away ones. It is also understandable that in the effort to Africanize the black American identity, some troublesome facts might be overlooked. As the year 2000 approached, this effort had blossomed into a comprehensive Afrocentric movement. The chief tenet of the movement was that in order to be mentally and emotionally whole, a black American had to be rooted in Africa and culturally African. Participants in the movement, then, concentrated on discovering African cultural elements in their own habits and incorporating new ones into their ways of life. American blacks were regarded as members of a diaspora of Africans. In part, this appeared to be an angry movement in which blacks alienated from America by the persistence of racism turned toward Africa.

Whether a large number of black Americans in the 1990s had accepted the Afrocentric framework was not clear. From slave times forward, many black Americans appeared to be Amerocentric in a sense truer than that in which whites were Amerocentric. Whites were Amerocentric in having found a new home in America. Blacks were Amerocentric in having been made in America. Slavery was a harrowing and transformational experience that, as biological fact, changed American blacks by mixing African gene lines and modifying them with infusions of European and Native American ancestry. As cultural fact, it cut them off from African traditions. The result was that black Americans, propelled by uncertain identities, had begun to invent new cultures long before emancipation. They used elements at hand, some African, some European, some Native American; and the results were coherent, vital, and more genuinely American than any other cultures in the United States, except those of Native Americans. As a result, black Americans already had been Afrocentric, Eurocentric, and Natively Amerocentric for centuries.

In short, black Americans in large numbers survived the harrowing experience and met the identity challenge by moving far forward in creating Amerocentric cultures. Almost no blacks were mainly Eurocentric, even though none were mainly Afrocentric either. No logical step required blacks angry at recollections of slavery or at white racism to turn toward Africa. There was no need to turn anywhere; they had already created what they needed and were what they needed to be.

Few white Americans of the 1990s were descended from white participants in slavery. Most were descended from immigrants who arrived after slavery had ended. Nevertheless, many blacks held them all accountable. They did so because serious invasions of privacy produce boundless bitterness, and some of the new whites acted toward blacks in manners reminiscent of the old days before the new whites had arrived.

Few Africans of the 1990s were descended from black participants in the transatlantic slave trade. Nearly all black Americans completely absolved any who might have been. Crimes that do not include invasions of privacy slide rapidly into the past, except for programs of outright genocide.

The severe beating by white Los Angeles police officers of a black motorist, Rodney King, in 1991, recorded by a bystander on videotape and later broadcast nationally, was both revolting and affecting because the attack went beyond angry physical assault to become a pure invasion of privacy. The motorist's life was in danger, and this was surely frightening, but what was sickening about the attack was that, as it continued, its only motivation could have been to devalue the motorist by convincing him that his body was simply a bag of flesh that the participating police officers could make of what they wished. As a result, the attack was principally an invasion of privacy. For many blacks who saw the tape, the beating evoked the legacy of outrage inherited from slave times; and, as a result, instead of simply being an infuriating example of a kind of brutality that blacks sometimes visit on other blacks, and whites on other whites, it sounded the historical Klaxon.

Only the concept of an invasion of privacy can explain such reactions. For blacks still powerfully affected by slave history and its aftermath, conflicts with whites occurred not at the level of pushing and shoving, irritation and anger, but instead at a deeper level of humiliation, rape, nausea, and outrage. Vomit, not venom, fueled the kind of bitterness involved: It was a kind of bitterness only invasions of privacy can elicit.

The ten decades that followed emancipation were frequently punctuated by events resembling the beating of the Los Angeles motorist, but unlike in the Los Angeles of 1991, blacks then had little recourse. These were the decades of legal segregation during which blacks in much of the United States were systematically excluded from the better schools, land ownership, promising housing, and many employment possibilities. Many ethnic groups suffered similar exclusions, although none for longer or with more consistency than blacks. These exclusions represented justifiable grievances, but they were not invasions of privacy. The invasions were added to them: the activities of white supremacist groups, such as "night riding," lynchings and murders that became almost commonplace during the 1920s; picking on blacks as sport, making them look bad; seeking sexual favors under veiled threats or quid pro quo promises; abusing the servants; picking fights with blacks as coming-of-age exercises for young white men; brutalizing blacks under the cloak of official authority. Again, black Americans were not the only ethnic group to be subjected to such actions, but they endured these abuses for longer and with the slave centuries as a background.

Surely, even during slavery, many blacks were able to whittle out moments of privacy through cleverness, by exploiting the masters' dependence on them, and through behavioral standards developed in slave communities to afford some privacy. The descendants of these people comprise part of the large number of blacks who, as the turn of the twenty-first century approached, were indistinguishable from most whites in their demands for privacy, except perhaps in having a stronger appetite for it.

But other blacks continued to have little chance to develop an appetite. As the twentieth century closed, many black Americans lived in large, isolated urban communities in which privacy received little respect. These communities were as subject as any other to the widespread pressures hostile to privacy, and yet few who lived in them had a basis to resist the anti-privacy message of the late twentieth century. Many who lived in these communities did not expect privacy because they, their parents, or grandparents had moved directly from situations in which their aspirations for privacy had been frustrated for generations by white invasions of privacy and by poverty.

Poverty forced many to rely on government services, in return for which dossier information had to be provided. Poverty made for dense living conditions, as it always did, and exposed one to the scrutiny of others—urban crowding in poor neighborhoods was an important reason why no urban poor had participated in the golden age of privacy. Crime was frequent in these communities; therefore, the police presence was heavy. It was difficult for anyone to avoid encounters with the law, and these encounters created police records that, after the 1980s, were centrally computerized and internationally available. Economic uncertainty made credit risks of many, and credit-rating services reported their information widely. Credit was often the only way to smooth out the uneven income flow that characterized life in these communities. Many children, growing up under stress, were problem children and were so recorded in school records widely available to others. Privacy was seriously compromised by crowding in residences, in buildings, and in schools. It was compromised by bullying behavior and child abuse, which thrived among desperate people. In addition, raw physical intrusions could not be avoided. People were crowded and noisy, rape was prevalent, burglary was frequent.

In addition, those from outside the communities did not often extend it: civil servants, police officers, bill collectors, landlords, or employers. Neither did those inside the communities. In fact, trouble, ugly and violent, too often resulted from the constant struggle to get some respect.

According to George Steiner, in the late twentieth century often the only privacy available was in madness or addiction.[11] Steiner was talking about the loss of privacy in general society, not in poor urban black communities where the loss was greater. It was no wonder that drug use became widespread there. Drug-induced states provided the only quiet moments. For many, they probably were the whole of privacy.

Here, then, were people who needed privacy as much as everyone else; yet many of them were farther from privacy than most members of other American ethnic groups.

The historical invasions of privacy visited upon some blacks had deprived them of a chance to develop a demand for privacy. As a result, they went into the end of the century with little resistance to further loss. In whites who were slipping into a condition in which "everything was shouted and nothing could be said in a quiet voice," to paraphrase Steiner,[12] presumably there was at least an awareness that what was being discarded need not be lost.

As the twentieth century closed, most black Americans did not live in desperate, isolated, low-privacy communities, but many did. The lives of persons in these communities could be better understood when the privacy factor was taken into consideration.

The race issue, then, was at least in part a privacy issue. The history of the mistreatment of blacks in the Americas and of their continuing responses to it could not be understood without reference to invasions of privacy.

Having been deprived of privacy for so long, many black Americans probably valued it more than many whites did. The most isolated blacks in the United States desperately needed privacy but had little chance of getting much. Yet most black Americans appeared to be like most white Americans as the end of the century approached. Their predecessors may not have participated in the nineteenth-century golden age of privacy, but they retained an appreciation of privacy despite the invasions during decades of slavery and segregation. They quickly realized that aspirations for privacy protection could be satisfied. As a result, Afrocentric or Amerocentric, most blacks belonged to the constituency that called for privacy.

WHITE POOR

The other large group left out of the nineteenth-century golden age of privacy was the white poor.[13] The chief reason the white poor lacked privacy or an interest in it was the same reason all poor tend to be indifferent: They had more pressing concerns. Privacy, as important as it is, looks like a luxury when viewed by those struggling for subsistence. Some forms of privacy are not luxuries, but instead are essentials for everyone: freedom from sexual abuse, for example. Others, such as finding quiet moments in which to develop one's thoughts, may seem less important and beyond expectation if one belongs to a large family in a small apartment in a crowded neighborhood. The urban poor in particular will find privacy inappropriate as a concern, even though poor individuals might fight every day to be let alone for a few minutes.

For the rural poor, opportunities for privacy resemble those of rural and village people everywhere from the time people first began to gather in organized settlements. Rural poverty is close to the timeless style of human life, at least of the life that became timeless when the Neolithic age brought geographic permanence. In rural poverty people come closest to the prehistoric and early historic manner of life, which is the kind most widely shared by the world's peoples. In this kind of life, the circle of relationships and activities in a village or town almost completely eliminates the features of privacy toward which twentieth-century people aspire. In the village, everyone knows everyone else. In addition, everyone knows everyone else's personal business: health problems, discord between husband and wife, unruly children, unrequited loves of sons or daughters, drunkenness, penchant for violence, disputes with neighbors, roving eye, jealousies, ambitions for wealth or power, laziness, penchant for insanity, tendency to cry, inability to shake off a loss, unreasonable hatreds, adoration of wife or husband, insecurities about abilities, pride, toughness under fire. There are no secrets. Encounters are witnessed and overheard. Other people intrude or offer advice or criticism. Privacy as control over others' access to information about oneself, in effect, does not exist, except for the extraordinarily clever. Privacy as safety-valve does not exist because everyone else learns what goes on in the small groups that would otherwise be safety-valve groups. Privacy as room to grow is hard to find because life is a tight web of interactions. Only privacy as respect is available, but only for those worthy of respect; but perhaps its availability is what makes the absence of the other forms tolerable.

However, because the setting is rural, quiet places can be found. Lovers may not be able to keep an affair unknown in the village, but they can find places to conduct it where they will not be seen. Similarly, a person who wants to be alone can go out and be alone. Rural settings do provide opportunities for physical privacy that compensate for the density of relationships and meddling in villages and towns.

The rural white poor of the United States had this timeless country privacy available. So did the black poor who were not enslaved, or had been liberated, except that some of the black rural poor were targeted for humiliation or terror of which invasions of privacy played an essential part. The white rural poor, then, faced the timeless village deprivations of privacy but enjoyed the timeless rural availability of privacy. But they took the latter for granted or neglected to call for more because they had more pressing concerns. These were the concerns of poverty: how to adequately stock the larder; how to manage serious illness without skilled medical assistance; how to rise above the fear of starvation or illness; how to pay off debts; how to husband the energy to get through the necessary work; how to shake off the despair of going nowhere; how to shake off the guilt at being unable to do more for your children; how to appease landowners or others controlling your livelihood; how to coax another year from worn out equipment; how to find a job. The rural poor in the nineteenth and in the twentieth century were close to a timeless form of life in which appreciation of privacy as an individual right did not play a part.

The urban poor had similar preoccupations. Most were never more than a few generations from rural poverty. At the start of the industrial revolution, the rural poor began to arrive in cities in large numbers and continued to do so until the late twentieth century: English peasantry migrated to the original mill towns; European peasants voyaged to American cities; rural Southern black poor moved to northern American cities.

In the cities, they lost the timeless rural type of compensating privacy. In the nineteenth century they became the industrial lower class. They worked long hours in factories and lived in compounds owned and controlled by the entrepreneurs who employed them. They were the urban proletariat, whose plight in Europe moved Karl Marx to draft the theories of communism that profoundly influenced global affairs to the end of the twentieth century. From the Marxist perspective, the nineteenth-century golden age of privacy was a luxury skimmed off the wealth produced through the exploitation of this proletariat.

The golden age was, in fact, made possible by increased wealth. Its features were bigger houses with separate rooms, larger lots, family wherewithal adequate to release families from dependence on the commonality, educational or self-improvement aspirations that supported the appropriation of solitary time for reading or study, upward mobility in which greater distance from the rabble was possible.

Whether Marx was right that the wealth was stolen from the urban poor, or whether the wealth accrued more positively from entrepreneurship or meliorism, it was true that the nineteenth-century golden age of privacy was based on increased wealth and that the urban poor were left out of it. In a sense, the lives of the urban poor, most of them white, were as bad as those of blacks in slavery or those newly emancipated. The urban poor did not have much more freedom of mobility, and no more health, wealth, or prospects. They were freer from directed assaults on what privacy they had, but they were as isolated as poor blacks from the development of privacy as a value.

As the twentieth century closed, the American white poor generally did not live conspicuously massed in urban neighborhoods like the black poor did. Many were rural poor. But there were many poor white people, almost 20.8 million by almanac count in 1992, that is, 10 percent of white Americans. By contrast, almost 31 percent of blacks and over 26 percent of Hispanics lived in poverty, according to almanac figures; but over twice as many whites as blacks were poor, and almost four times as many whites as Hispanics.[14] One cannot conclude with certainty that the white poor of the later twentieth century were the descendants of the white poor of the nineteenth or eighteenth centuries, as one can ascertain that the black poor of the twentieth century were descended from the black poor of previous centuries. But many poor whites probably had roots in earlier poverty. Those who had such roots had been discouraged for at least a century and a half from developing an interest in privacy.

Poverty, then, like race, has been in part a problem of invasions of privacy. Lack of privacy is a condition of poverty; and the poor who lose hope give up, among other things, the aspiration to satisfy their need for privacy. One way to distinguish people who are lost to the cycle of poverty from those who are poor of circumstance but not of spirit is to realize that the former have ceased to demand, take, or pursue privacy in their daily lives. The latter, on the other hand, act as though they deserve privacy even if their circumstances make it unavailable.

NOTES

1. Edward Shils, *Center and Periphery: Essays in Macrosociology* (Chicago: University of Chicago Press, 1975), p. 323.

2. Maxine Van de Wetering, "The Popular Concept of 'Home' in Nineteenth Century America," *Journal of American Studies* 18, no. 1 (1984); 5–28.

3. These torts are those of physical intrusion upon a person's private space; inaccurate portrayal of a person publicly so as to put the person in a false light; public disclosure of embarrassing private facts; and, appropriating a person's likeness for commercial gain. The four were first outlined as distinct torts by William Prosser in a 1960 law review article. William Prosser, "Privacy," *California Law Review* 48 (1960); 383. Some states recognize all four; other states, two or three; a few states, none. About a dozen states recognize the torts by statute; the remainder recognize them in common law.

4. The U.S. Supreme Court ruled in *Griswold v. Connecticut*, 381 U.S. 479 (1965), that a privacy right protecting the body and body-related matters from government invasion was implied by the First, Third, Fourth, Fifth, and Ninth amendments.

5. Pub. L. 93-579, 88 Stat. 1986 (effective, Sept. 27, 1975), 5 U.S.C.A. sec. 552b.

6. 15 U.S.C.A. sections 1681-1681s.

7. Some black Americans have applauded these traditional societies for being refreshingly non-individualistic.

8. According to the 1992 *World Almanac and Book of Facts,* the population density of Nigeria was 322 per square mile; Sierra Leone, 154; Senegal, 101; Tanzania, 67; Togo, 158; Uganda, 180; Zaire, 37; Mali, 17; Liberia, 66;, Kenya, 105. By contrast, that of France was 252; Denmark, 308; Cuba, 239; Germany, 221; India, 666; Japan, 844; the United Kingdom, 601; Massachusetts, 767; Illinois, 206. From 1995 to 2025, the population of Kenya is expected to increase from 31.4 million to 82.9; of Uganda from 22.5 to 52.3 million; of Zaire from 44.8 to 104.4 million; of Nigeria from 135.5 to 338.1 million; of Senegal from 8.7 to 18.9 million. These figures do not include adjustments for the AIDS epidemic.

9. See David Flaherty, *Privacy in Colonial New England* (Charlottesville: University of Virginia Press, 1972).

10. See John Kells Ingram, of Trinity College, Dublin, writing in

Encyclopaedia Britannica, 1959, entry for "Slavery." See also James A. Rawley, *The Transatlantic Slave Trade* (New York: Norton, 1981), pp. 267–281. See also Edward Reynolds, *Stand The Storm* (New York: Allison and Busby, 1985), pp. 33–46. Reynolds included an account indicating that in the nineteenth century, 34 percent of slaves sold by Africans to Europeans were war captives, 30 percent had been kidnapped, 7 percent had been sold by relatives or superiors, 7 percent had been sold because of their debts, 11 percent had been condemned to slavery by judicial process, and 11 percent were in slavery for unspecified reasons (Ibid., p. 33).

11. George Steiner, "Night Words," in George Steiner, *Language and Silence* (New York: Atheneum, 1967).

12. Ibid.

13. Poor white families that remained consistently poor from the early nineteenth into the late twentieth century were cut off from the issue of privacy protection as much as were poor black families.

14. *The World Almanac and Book of Facts 1992.*

Chapter 4

Types of Privacy

Those who have tried to write philosophies of privacy have been particular about definitions, some unwilling to include all manifestations of privacy in a working definition. The objective of philosophical definitions of privacy has been to produce standards for legal judgment and non-legal ethical decision making. Philosophers have been reluctant to embrace the concept of privacy.

The philosophical approach to privacy favored by Ruth Gavison involves restricting the definition of privacy to matters of accessibility to a person, omitting from the concept much that is widely considered to be private or to touch upon privacy, such as sex-related regulations, dress codes, or noise pollution nuisances.[1] Sissela Bok also has focused on the access factor, defining privacy "as the condition of being protected from unwanted access by others—either physical access, personal information, or attention. Claims to privacy are claims to control access to what one takes—however grandiosely—to be one's personal domain."[2] Similarly, Hyman Gross has written, "Loss of privacy occurs when the limits one has set on acquaintance with his personal affairs are not respected."[3]

Problems arise when the definition of privacy is narrowed so much that it includes only matters pertaining to access to a person. For example, Gavison lists as exclusions from the privacy concept insulting, harassing, or persecuting behavior; unsolicited mail and phone calls; and exposure to noises, smells, and sights.[4] Some actions that fall into these categories can reasonably be understood to be access to a person, particularly where access is defined as Gavison does, as physical access and attention as well as access to information about the person. As a result, this resolution of the definitional problem raises other problems.

However, the objective of limiting the definition of privacy to access is clear. It is to remove the concept of privacy from matters related to the regulation of what many people consider to be personal preferences. In terms of this objective, the right to abortion should not be founded on the privacy concept, nor should privacy be included in the formula of any analysis or decision making with respect to the regulation of birth control or sexual behavior. In this view, regulation of a personal zone can be distinguished from access to it—certainly from access to information about it—and should be approached through a standard different from privacy—such as autonomy. For example, Gross has criticized the 1965 *Griswold* decision, in which the U.S. Supreme Court invalidated a statutory prohibition on the distribution of birth control information to married couples.[5] The Court found that privacy rights were violated. Gross disagreed. What was offended there, he said, was the autonomy of couples from government meddling, not their privacy, because the state did not seek to become acquainted with the couples, only to regulate their personal affairs.[6] According to Gross, the Court "muddied the waters" by handling *Griswold* as a privacy case.[7]

However, other writers have defined privacy to include regulation of a personal zone. Walter F. Pratt, writing on privacy in Britain, offered a double definition: privacy is the right of an individual to control information about himself and the right to a private sphere.[8] M. C. Slough wrote that privacy was the right to live at least part of one's life divorced from public interest and the public eye, to live according to one's own indi-

vidual choice and free from the probing of other people.[9] Those
adopting Slough's definition would endorse the use of the privacy concept to restrict the regulation of behavior within a personal zone. Pratt's definition seems to have the same meaning
as Slough's even though some readers might interpret the
words "private sphere" to refer only to a private informational
sphere, not to one of choices and action.

Other writers have focused their definitions on the element
of personal control more than on any particular personal area
in which such control might become important. For example,
Robert Ellis Smith has written:

> Control. . . . Privacy is the right to control your own body,
> as in the right to an abortion or the right to whatever sex-
> ual activities you choose. Privacy is the right to control
> your own living space, as in the right to be free from un-
> reasonable searches and seizures. Privacy is the right to
> control your own identity, as in the right to be known by
> a name of your choice and not a number, the right to
> choose your own hair and dress styles, the right to per-
> sonality. Privacy is the right to control information about
> yourself, as in the right to prevent disclosure of private
> facts or the right to know which information is kept on
> you and how it is used.[10]

According to Stephen T. Margulis, "Privacy, as a whole or in
part, represents the control of transactions between person(s)
and other(s), the ultimate aim of which is to enhance autonomy
and/or to minimize vulnerability."[11]

Definitions based on control are more comprehensive than
those based on access to personal information. But the control-
based definitions may be so comprehensive as to be unmanageable as tools for law, policy, or ethics; this is what proponents
of the information access definitions assert. However, the con-
trol-based definitions are enlightening—good reminders of
what is at stake—and may appear to be unmanageable only because we are still uncomfortable turning over a broad spectrum
of our moral thought to a concept ignored by famous philoso-

phers and that has been taken seriously for only 100 years—
and very seriously only for about 40 years.

Robert Ellis Smith has offered a universal warning to those
seeking to define privacy. Do not equate privacy with solitude,
loneliness, or introversion, he cautioned. "Gregarious people
seek privacy. They like to be with other people, but they like
also to control what these other people know about them. Don't
equate privacy with secretiveness or concealment. People who
honestly and candidly disclose everything about themselves
seek privacy. They want to make sure their personal freedom,
their autonomy, is not restricted by what they have revealed
about themselves."[12] Similarly, Bok has warned that secrecy is
not the only way to protect privacy, and non-private matters
may be kept secret.[13] Gross noted that "an offense to privacy is
an offense to autonomy, but not all offenses to autonomy are
offenses to privacy."[14]

These warnings indicate agreement that definitions of privacy should distinguish privacy from related concepts with
which it overlaps, such as solitude, secrecy, autonomy, liberty,
or being let alone. However, no definition of privacy cleanly
escapes from entanglement with some other concept. Defined
as a limitation on informational access, privacy resembles secrecy. Defined as a limitation on physical or attentional access,
it resembles solitude or being let alone. Defined as freedom
from regulation, it resembles autonomy. It is for this reason
that McCloskey has argued that English law should not be
changed to recognize a privacy right. Privacy, he said, has no
intrinsic value as a basic right and can, at best, be derived from
other rights.[15]

Those interested in protecting or understanding privacy face
a major contradiction. On the one hand, there is a nearly universal, and apparently timeless, constituency in favor of privacy. Signs of this constituency appear in the anthropological
and historical records. In addition, the experienced needs of
daily life provide most people with additional signs. People
need moments to themselves. They prefer public bathrooms
when no one else is in them. They need to be alone to concen-
trate on difficult projects or mastering techniques, learning, or
writing. They close the curtains before undressing, and so on.

On the other hand, the attitudes and conclusions of philosophical writers are negative toward privacy, as if to say that what is obvious to everyone else does not exist. Those philosophers of privacy who do not deny privacy an independent existence narrow its meaning so much that it becomes unrecognizable except to initiates in legal or moral philosophy.

The work of psychologists may help resolve this contradiction. Psychologists appear to acknowledge the ambivalence in philosophical circles; yet their own evidence and theories tend to support the common understanding that privacy in its comprehensive range is important. In addition, they tend to break down privacy into types and functions, producing a defined, though complex, picture to replace the conceptual soup that seems to distress the philosophers.

Alan F. Westin, in his influential *Privacy and Freedom*, published in 1967, identified four functions of privacy: (1) personal autonomy, which is individual control over when to go public; (2) emotional release, which is respite from emotional stimulation and room to set aside social roles; (3) self-evaluation, which is room to integrate experiences in a meaningful pattern, particularly necessary for creative work; and, (4) limited and protected communication, room to share candid communication, confidences and intimacies with trusted persons.[16] Similarly, Irwin Altman has described the functions of privacy as follows: (1) personal-boundary control for self-definition; (2) room to evaluate oneself, others, and new situations; and, (3) respect for the value of the self, to enhance self-identity.[17]

According to Carl D. Schneider, privacy provides the following: (1) depth of life—what is always in public is shallow, he said; (2) free selves to occupy the public realm—without privacy, persons do not develop the strength to act in public, he suggested; and, (3) space for essential mysteries and body-boundaries—he cited Biblical admonitions to pray alone, fast alone, and not make a show of one's religion, as underlining the importance of this space.[18] Schneider also said that privacy serves as a safety valve, by providing room to drop roles and recuperate from encounters with "unbearable" people.[19]

Culling through these three reviews of privacy's functions,

one finds considerable agreement and can extract four distinct types of privacy. One is privacy as access control: controlling one's personal boundaries and the release of one's secrets; not having one's mask stripped away. Another is privacy as room to grow: cultivating interior processes for understanding, enrichment, and integration of character and personality; and sharing the same with trusted others. A third is privacy as a safety valve: resting and recuperating from the public arena. A fourth is privacy as respect for the individual: insisting that one is more than a cipher and respecting others for being more than ciphers.

These four definitions are philosophically manageable. They are distinct and might be placed in rank by order of importance. They might be argued to all have intrinsic value, or only instrumental value, or be distinguished from one another for the assignment of value. They can be used as standards against which to measure community customs, institutional policies, or legal protections. These types of privacy are reasonably thorough in providing categories for most known types of privacy.

Of the first of the four—access-control privacy—Altman commented, "Across societies there appears to be a mix of different modes of behavior—environmental, verbal, non-verbal, and psychological—that assist in the regulation of interaction." These, he said, are used to achieve "changing balances of openness/closedness and accessibility/inaccessibility to others."[20] One environmental device, he said, was clothing, as in dressing formally or using a veil. Another was in regulating physical distance from others; another was the use of doors, screens, and walls. Examples of culturally based devices, he said, were the sanctity of the closed bathroom door, urban street manners, and etiquette. Non-verbal devices included postures, orientations in space, facial expressions, and bodily tension. Verbal devices included such comments as "Leave me alone now" and "You're too noisy," plus intonation and, when possible, switching to a second language or, if you are a child, pig Latin.[21] Needless to say, everyone is busy all day with some of these access-control devices.

Barry Schwartz has commented regarding access-control privacy: "Guarantees of privacy, that is, rules as to who may and who may not observe or reveal information about whom, must be established in any stable social system. If these assurances do not prevail—if there is normlessness with respect to privacy—every withdrawal from visibility may be accompanied by a measure of espionage, for without rules to the contrary, persons are naturally given to intrude upon [in]visibility."[22]

Schwartz noted that privacy—in the sense of access control—has been a privilege of those of higher status and has been a luxury, while the right to invade the privacy of others has also been a status symbol.[23] Other writers have noted that a need for privacy—in all forms—has been a characteristic of the upper and upper middle classes.[24]

Access-control privacy and secrecy are closely related concepts, Bok has pointed out, particularly "where secrecy guards against unwanted access by others—against their coming too near, learning too much, observing too closely."[25] In fact, she said, privacy is the part of life for which secrecy is regarded as most indispensable—so much so that in secularized Western societies, privacy and secrecy are sometimes mistaken for each other. In distinguishing between the concepts, she noted that non-private matters too can be kept secret.[26] Her comments are reminders that to endorse access-control privacy is also to endorse hiding and secrecy because these are principal means for controlling access. They are also measures with negative connotations. Carol Warren and Barbara Laslett have pointed out that privacy is consensually supported, whereas secrecy is not.[27] That hiding and secrecy are advanced when privacy is endorsed is probably one factor causing some philosophical writers to refuse to heartily support privacy.

According to Sidney M. Jourard, "Privacy is experienced as 'room to grow in.' "[28] People disclose their selves, he wrote, only under conditions of trust and privacy. However, when people disclose themselves to one another in privacy, "a secret society comes into existence." This, he said, is discouraging to those running institutions that seek to control their members; as a result, such institutions prefer non-privacy.[29] Regarding privacy as room to grow, Yehudi Cohen noted: "Healthy and mature identification is never complete; no society could function and survive if the people in it felt completely fused with one another. Some degree of separateness and insularity is necessary in every individual if he is going to develop and mature."[30]

In writing about solitude, Anthony Storr was also discussing privacy as room to grow. In fact, this second form of privacy—room to grow—finds solitude to be a principal device, just as access-control privacy finds secrecy to be a device. Thinking, Storr wrote, is predominantly a solitary activity, as is prayer: "It appears, therefore, that some development of the capacity to be alone is necessary if the brain is to function at its best, and if the individual is to fulfil his highest potential. Human beings easily become alienated from their own deepest needs and feelings. Learning, thinking, innovation, and maintaining contact with one's own inner world are all facilitated by solitude."[31]

A third form of privacy—privacy as safety valve—is the finding of places of respite. According to Jourard, private places are needed if people are to maintain psychological health—places to "be rather than be respectable."[32] Such places can be hard to find, he said, due to urbanization and to the spread of institutional standards that tend to keep people in professional or career roles all the time. Such places are needed, he said, because when roles do not fit, people have limited choices: They can either reject the roles and be labelled crazy; conceal their discontentment and risk breakdown; or discard the roles in private places.[33] Westin suggested that social roles can be sustained only for limited periods of time. In setting them aside, he said, people sometimes need room in which to break minor norms and to ignore etiquette, room in which to blow off steam at authorities and launch even unfair and unreasonable criticisms.[34]

Privacy as respect, a fourth form of privacy, is the kind of privacy whose violation may elicit shame or embarrassment. According to Schneider, symbols of the individual, such as a name, face, or body, cannot be encroached upon without giving offense or causing shame.[35] Slapping or spitting in a person's face comes to mind, as does joking about an unusual name, drawing a likeness then marring it, or hanging an effigy. Exposure to view of certain bodily functions (defecating, suffering great pain, dying, sexual activity, sleep), said Schneider, tends to degrade the individual by reducing him to a mere physical entity. Such exposure, he suggested, is the essence of obscenity.[36] Doors exist, said Schwartz, because people have a sense of self-integrity.[37]

Another writer, Jeffrey H. Reiman, has regarded the principle of respect to be the cornerstone of privacy—in particular, respect for persons as choosers.[38] Reiman helps explain one paradox of privacy, namely that privacy is public, that it is not aloneness or loneliness but that instead it exists in relationship with a public, a community. "Privacy," said Reiman, "is a social ritual by means of which an individual's moral title to his existence is conferred, . . . by means of which the social group recognizes—and communicates to the individual—that his existence is his own."[39]

Some acts violate several of these four types of privacy simultaneously. One example is rape, which violates privacy as access control and privacy as respect for the individual. Apparently, a rapist's motivation is, in part, to injure the victim by destroying his or her confidence in controlling access and to insult the person through disrespect. Probably, some of the perpetrators have themselves been victims of invasions, sexual or non-sexual, and commit their rapes to pass the insults along. The shame reaction to the invasion of respect has been a major obstacle to rape reporting and prosecution. However, the growing intolerance for rape and sensitivity to victims' reactions are signs of recent advances in support for privacy in the moral lives of several societies.

A more positive example of behavior that violates several kinds of privacy at once is military boot camp. Here all four versions of privacy are invaded, definitely but not extremely, and only for a term, for the instrumentally still acceptable objective of bending people to accept uniformity and control by others when they are on duty as soldiers. Recently, similar training has been reported to be effective in rehabilitating delinquents.[40]

Those who balk at endorsing privacy do so in much the same spirit in which a drill instructor would balk at overvaluing privacy during basic training. They surmise that a higher end can be served by suppressing privacy.[41] According to Schneider, "[M]any regard the private life with suspicion as a retreat from the demanding but ultimately essential public realm."[42] Some, he said, even regard privacy as immoral, either as a fall from communal nature or as selfishness that must be restrained.[43]

At no point in the past century was hostility to privacy more boldly displayed than among young rebels of the 1960s and 1970s. John W. Chapman, writing in 1971, suggested that the moral psychology of the young at that time was a threat to privacy.[44] He asserted that student and radical movements were non-private and that privacy was an affront to what they were after; indeed, some practices of the times were non-private—for example, sex acts where others could see and hear; the blunt sexual overture to a near stranger, "Let's fuck"; casual nakedness; congested communes and "crashpads"; distrust and disrespect for private property. It is reasonably arguable that the waning of those movements resulted from a resurgence of the desire for privacy. Surely, this need destroyed the communes.

Nevertheless, remnants of the anti-privacy spirit that was strong in that period can be found in the ambivalent and cautious definitions of privacy offered by some writers. Even some philosophical proponents of privacy have exhibited this caution. Negley wrote: "[S]ome degree of privacy is necessary in order to ensure to the individual the possibility of moral choice and action; but this is too simple an answer."[45] A better answer he left for later moral definition and analysis. A value judgment must be made, he said, if privacy is to receive protection as a right. "If privacy is defined as an essential requirement for the achievement of morality, then privacy is a right that the law must protect and provide."[46]

Possibly, some of those who have insisted upon restrictive definitions of privacy would support some comprehensive definitions, if certain limitations were observed. For example, Gavison, who proposed that the definition of privacy be restricted, certainly in legal contexts, to access-control privacy, nevertheless offered a comprehensive list when discussing the instrumental value of privacy. She wrote: "It appears that privacy is central to the attainment of individual goals under every theory of the individual that has ever captured man's imagination."[47] She said that privacy frees individuals from physical access; prevents distraction in activities requiring concentration (learning, in particular); permits relaxation and intimacy; prevents discovery of knowledge about a person; promotes liberty of action by freeing a person from censure, ridicule, and pressure to conform; encourages people to dare more; and promotes mental health by relieving persons from pressure to conform.[48] This is a very ample statement of support for the four versions of privacy discussed above; and, if her conception of access-control privacy includes everything in this list, then she must be considered a proponent of a comprehensive privacy concept, even as she rejects legal protection of the whole of it.

Most commentators view privacy as a continuum. At one end, where individuals experience great privacy, there is madness. According to Ainslie H. Mears, nearly all schizophrenics are extreme introverts.[49] According to William E. Lyons, the result of too much privacy is madness, introversion exaggerated to the point of no connection with the outside world.[50] At the other end of the continuum is totalitarianism. To Robert Ellis Smith, retention of privacy is resistance to state control.[51] According to M. C. Slough, privacy can thrive only in a democratic society; the totalitarian mind does not respect privacy or any of its values.[52]

As a result, it is toward a balance that most commentators point. Packard noted: "We do not need to be anti-social to cherish privacy. Good citizens know they have responsibilities to their communities, and delight in filling them. But they also know they are better citizens if they can feel free to keep a part of their lives as uniquely their own."[53] Altman noted that the pursuit of optimization—not too much, not too little—is a feature of privacy.[54]

One obstacle to pursuing a comfortable balance is the view that privacy has no value as a concept but is instead secondarily derived from other concepts or rights, and, as a result, should not have status as a moral, legal, or policy standard. In response to this view, others have insisted upon paring down the privacy concept to the hard nut of access-control privacy, which appears to have immediate, concrete usefulness and therefore to be invulnerable to criticism. The pared down concept, however, is skimpy compared to what is commonly understood to be privacy. Fortunately, many commentators agree on a conception of privacy that is true to anthropological and historical evidence and also to common understanding.

NOTES

1. Ruth Gavison, "Privacy and the Limits of Law," *Yale Law Journal* 89 (1980); 436.

2. Sissela Bok, *Secrets* (New York: Pantheon, 1982), p. 11.

3. Hyman Gross, "Privacy and Autonomy," in J. Roland Pennock and John W. Chapman, *Privacy* (New York: Atherton, 1971), p. 170.

4. Gavison, "Privacy," p. 436.

5. *Griswold v. Connecticut*, 381 U.S. 479 (1965).

6. Gross, "Privacy and Autonomy," in Pennock and Chapman, *Privacy*, p. 436.

7. Ibid.

8. Walter F. Pratt, *Privacy in Britain* (Lewisburg, PA: Bucknell University Press, 1975), p. 13.

9. M. C. Slough, *Privacy, Freedom and Responsibility* (Springfield, IL: Thomas, 1969), p. 3.

10. Robert Ellis Smith, *Privacy* (Garden City, NY: Archer/Doubleday, 1979), p. 323.

11. Stephen T. Margulis, "Conceptions of Privacy," *Journal of Social Issues* 33, no. 3 (1977); 10.

12. Smith, *Privacy*, p. 317.

13. Bok, *Secrets*, p. 11.

14. Gross, "Privacy and Autonomy," in Pennock and Chapman, *Privacy*, p. 181.

15. H. J. McCloskey, "Privacy and the Right to Privacy," *Philosophy* 55 (1980); 17–38.

16. Alan Westin, *Privacy and Freedom* (New York: Atheneum, 1967), pp. 33–39.

17. Irwin Altman, *The Environment and Social Behavior: Privacy, Personal Space, Territory, Crowding* (Monterey, CA: Brooks/Cole, 1975), pp. 45–51.

18. Carl D. Schneider, *Shame, Exposure and Privacy* (Boston: Beacon, 1977), pp. 42–43.

19. Ibid., p. 41.

20. Altman, *Environment and Social Behavior*, p. 16.

21. Ibid., pp. 32–42.

22. Barry Schwartz, "The Social Psychology of Privacy," *American Journal of Sociology* 73, no. 6 (1968); 742.

23. Ibid., p. 743.

24. See Edward Banfield, *The Unheavenly City* (Boston: Little, Brown, 1970); and Paul Fussell, *Class* (New York: Ballantine, 1983).

25. Bok, *Secrets*, p. 13.

26. Ibid., pp. 7–11.

27. Carol Warren, and Barbara Laslett, "Privacy and Secrecy," *Journal of Social Issues* 33, no. 3 (1979); 43–51.

28. Sidney M. Jourard, "Psychological Aspects of Privacy," *Law and Contemporary Problems* 1, no. 2 (Spring 1966); 318.

29. Ibid., p. 313.

30. Yehudi A. Cohen, *The Transition From Childhood to Adolescence* (Chicago: Aldine, 1964), pp. 25–26.

31. Anthony Storr, *Solitude* (New York: Free Press, 1988), p. 28.

32. Jourard, "Psychological Aspects," p. 310.

33. Ibid., pp. 309–310.

34. Westin, *Privacy*, pp. 35–36.

35. Schneider, *Shame, Exposure and Privacy*, pp. 49–51.

36. Ibid.

37. Schwartz, "The Social Psychology of Privacy," p. 747.

38. Jeffrey H. Reiman, "Privacy, Intimacy, and Personhood," *Philosophy and Public Affairs* 6 (1976); 26–44.

39. Ibid., p. 39.

40. See Bill Turque with David L. Gonzalez and Frank Washington, "Experiments in Boot Camp," *Newsweek* (May 22, 1989); pp. 42–43. Presumably, under training conditions the delinquents can be shown that they have skills and traits they didn't know they had, and these discoveries become grounds for self-respect and positive identity after the training ends.

41. A drill instructor, of course, might value privacy, except during training and other exercises; and the military makes sure that its officers have some privacy.

42. Schneider, *Shame, Exposure and Privacy*, p. 41.

43. Ibid.

44. John W. Chapman, "Personality and Privacy," in J. Roland Pennock and John W. Chapman, *Privacy* (New York: Atherton, 1971), pp. 236–255.

45. Glenn Negley, "Philosophical Views on the Value of Privacy," *Law and Contemporary Problems* 1, no. 2 (Spring 1966); 319.

46. Ibid., p. 325.

47. Ruth Gavison, "Privacy and the Limits of Law," p. 445.

48. Ibid., pp. 446–449.

49. Ainslie Meares, *The Introvert* (Springfield, IL: Thomas, 1958), p. 4.

50. William E. Lyons, *The Disappearance of Introspection* (Cambridge: MIT Press, 1986), p. 144.

51. Smith, *Privacy*, p. 327.

52. Slough, *Privacy, Freedom and Responsibility*, p. 13.

53. Vance Packard, *The Naked Society* (New York: D. McKay, 1964), p. 337.

54. Altman, *Environment and Social Behavior*, p. 25.

_____ Chapter 5 _____

The Pernicious Side of Privacy

Privacy clearly is not an unqualified good. It is a need that must be satisfied. Just as the need for food can be oversatisfied, so can the need for privacy. We need enough, but not too much. One way to get at the nature of privacy is to consider what is too much.

Schizophrenia appears to be linked to a great excess of privacy. One writer has suggested that it amounts to an inadequate and inappropriate device of access control possibly developed as a response to invasions of privacy at crucial stages of growing up.[1] But short of schizophrenia—which recent research suggests may be a chemical problem, with excess privacy a consequence—what are the negative results of too much privacy?

ACCESS-CONTROL PRIVACY

An excess of privacy as access control makes an eccentric of a person in his or her individual experience and a mystery of the person in the community. To live fruitfully with others, a person must be known by them. The three components of access must be present. Others must be able to physically reach the person; they must have an opportunity to observe the person; and they must have information about the person. They cannot be asked to draw close to a person without knowledge of that person. Human beings are dangerous to one another, and others need information in order to put uncertainty to rest. In addition, people crave friendship and must be given the opportunity, which only information and contact can provide, of mining friendships out of possible contacts. Furthermore, most people crave productive interaction. For some, the goals of such interaction are merely conversational, but for others the goals are the performance of tasks. Productive interaction requires that people be placed in a mosaic of complementary roles, and such assignments, either formal or informal, cannot be made without information about the persons involved. An excess of access-control privacy, then, deprives the individual of satisfaction of his other cravings; and it deprives the community of a member.

People shrouded in mystery, it should be remembered, are not treated merely as curiosities; in most communities, they are feared. They make others uncomfortable, and they are vulnerable to scapegoating. Mysteriousness sounds unpleasant notes that touch everyone, and the tune can turn out badly for the recluse. Such is human nature. It might be suggested that the problems of reclusive status exist only in small towns and villages, that cities provide anonymity that denatures the problem; but this is not altogether true. In cities, one does not expect to know many of the others one sees, but we do expect others to belong to communities, communities on top of communities, circles on top of circles. Indeed, in a city, there is more room for a person to live without a circle. But the neighborhoods of such people—the realm of the transient—are typically seedy and violent. One is reminded of Jivaro society as described by Moore: no public realm, only private; no community or clan, only families; no trust and little requirement to interact, and disagreements settled through violence.[2] One is also reminded of the transient cow towns of the nineteenth-century American West.

An excess of access-control privacy, then, creates either the tension that comes from having unknowns in a community, or the instability that results when all community units are private. To achieve a balance, a community must either decline to give full control over access to individuals or educate individuals to use their control with the community in mind.

At least two factors must be considered with regard to access-control privacy: how much control individuals have over access to themselves; and how much of this control is actually used by them to deny access to themselves. If individuals have 100 percent control over access, yet do not isolate themselves, then neither the society nor the individuals suffer from an excess of this kind of privacy. If the society gives 100 percent control and individuals isolate themselves as much as possible, then the society and the individuals suffer. If individuals have 50 percent control and isolate themselves as much as they can, the society may not have an excess.

ROOM-TO-GROW PRIVACY

An excess of privacy as room to grow does not at first glance seem bad at all. Certainly, some people need much of it during critical periods of life: the teenager hanging out in his room, the grieving person, the recently fired person planning career strategies, the victim shaking off a sense of vulnerability. One hesitates to recommend any perspective that would curtail opportunities for this kind of private adjustment. Also needing much of this kind of privacy are those who must work alone: artists, craftsmen and artisans; writers; scholars; students in every field. For some of these people, "the more, the better" seems to be the operative rule regarding room-to-grow privacy.

People availing themselves of privacy as room to grow may need to be free of interruptions, but they do not have to sharply limit observation by others or the flow of information about themselves. Privacy as room to grow is really time without distraction. It can be had in a crowded room as well as in an empty one. It can be had even if the person occasionally distributes pieces of highly intimate information about himself. As a result, an extreme of this kind of privacy does not appear to carry the same threat to community integrity that an excess of access-control privacy carries.

However, a person who withdraws deeply into room-to-grow privacy risks never returning, or may fail to meet his own needs or to perform the tasks others rely upon him to perform. These are the negatives of privacy as room to grow. Also, this kind of privacy can wound individuals and fatigue a community, as will be discussed below.

SAFETY-VALVE PRIVACY

Safety-valve privacy is unlike room-to-grow privacy in that it does not require as much solitude. The typical person seeking privacy as room to grow wants to be alone or with one or two intimate friends; but a person seeking privacy as a safety valve can be with a group. This form of privacy provides a place to drop oppressive roles and to recover from encounters with difficult people. For many, safety-valve privacy is available at home with trustworthy family members. A favorite tavern can serve a similar function, as can an athletic club. Of course, one adopts roles in these venues too, and if any of these roles are arduous, relief from them may require that a person be alone. A certain amount of information control and freedom from observation may be needed to support this kind of privacy; statements may be made or activities pursued that a person would not want to have revealed.

One danger of this kind of privacy is that when the people who gather for this form of relief are consistent and uniform in what they seek relief from, they may become a nucleus of revolt—a secret society. This is a pernicious outcome for those who strive to control institutions, but the price of stifling safety-valve privacy may be to generate pressures that will cause social or political upheavals.

Persons who take this kind of privacy to excess may refuse to adopt public roles. This might create employment crises for these individuals. For a community, it might mean a decline of public spirit and a reduction in good works.

Safety-valve privacy is not operative every time friends or relatives get together, and it is not the usual cause for low community spirit; hopelessness unrelated to privacy is. Safety-valve privacy is, by definition, a response to discomfort in the roles people must adopt to make their ways in existing society. When people seek an excess of safety-valve privacy, something is wrong in the organization of the society. The formal role-life has failed to evolve as fast as individuals have changed or it has evolved rapidly where individuals cannot change. The roles become uncomfortable; privacy as safety valve becomes more important; time and energy invested in exercising this privacy increase; the privacy spawns secret societies that cause disruption and foment change. This process describes the history of the 1960s and early 1970s, during which dramatic changes occurred in the texture of American life regarding races and sexes, dress and grooming, attitudes to the body and its display, dietary latitude, and attitudes toward marital status and family composition. It also describes the history of the 1990s when many discovered that the changes begun in the 1960s had gone farther than they were willing or able to go.

As a result, it is difficult to describe an excess of safety-valve privacy as pernicious unless one is invested in controlling others to maintain a status quo. A natural balance occurs regarding this kind of privacy. An effort to restrict it when its importance increases is an effort to stifle a process by which a community meets its challenges—and this is more pernicious than room-to-grow privacy itself can ever be. Meanwhile, almost everywhere, some safety-valve privacy is needed because formal roles can never be made to fit perfectly and because we will always need relief from difficult people.

RESPECT PRIVACY

Privacy as respect can be taken too far. At an extreme, this kind of privacy would create a community in which conversation would always be platitudinous, encounters etiquette ridden, and news reporting shallow. Risks must be taken if communication is to have bite. One risk is that of treading upon private matters, causing discomfort or embarrassment. People can always tell you to mind your own business, but standards that require you entirely to avoid these risks impose restrictions on communications that are the pernicious side of privacy as respect.

Americans in the 1980s and 1990s are far from this kind of excess; we are not a delicate society and we expect people to withstand embarrassment without even showing it. Sensitivity to dignity values is low. Friends, parents, teachers, ministers, policemen, employers, and political figures get precious few opportunities to enjoy dignity. Privacy as respect is not excessive in late twentieth-century America. Our greater problem is that we do not provide enough of it.

Privacy is in part a negative concept. It shares an etymological root with "privation" and "deprivation." For most of human existence, privacy was one of the ordeals of solitary travel. For many of those who imposed agriculture and ranching on the American and Canadian West, it was one of the ordeals of life. Even now, in the Midwestern farm states, most farmsteads have a powerful lamp on a high post in the yard. The lamp is not there merely to illuminate the farmstead; it is there also so that the farmstead can be seen from other farmsteads. The lights are there so that one can look out at night over the flattish landscape and see dots of light at distant farmsteads and feel less alone.

We still use solitary confinement as a punishment, and most prisoners prefer the danger and brutality of communal convict life, with its insults, intimidations, fights, rapes, and killings, to forced privacy. We use silent treatment to impose privacy as a penalty on persons who commit unofficial crimes within or against our social groups. Privacy is for many an unpleasantness and for some a nightmare.

Indeed, privacy should be expected to have a negative element at its root because, according to psychologists, three-quarters of people are extroverted, and extroverts find some elements of privacy to be oppressive and exhausting. Extroverts need certain kinds of privacy, in particular, access-control privacy to limit the flow of information about them, safety-valve privacy as long as it can be shared with a group, and respect privacy. Yet when privacy requires solitude, it may lose its appeal for extroverts; and because the concept has always suggested, or threatened, solitude, it has always deserved its negative etymological link, as far as most people have been concerned. Extroverts' discomfort in being alone is perhaps privacy's most pernicious element—and one that is easily overlooked in discussions focused on privacy's role in community life or on its usefulness in moral or legal philosophy. "People who need people" are hurt by any more than a little privacy.

The essence of extroversion, according to David Keirsey and Marilyn Bates, is that extroverts draw energy from others.[3] "Talking to people, playing with people, and working with people is what charges their batteries. Extraverts experience loneliness when they are not in contact with people. When an extreme extravert leaves a party at two o'clock in the morning, he may well be ready to go to another one. His batteries are almost overcharged, having received so much energy from the interaction," Keirsey and Bates have written.[4] According to Carl Jung, a widely influential psychologist of the early twentieth century, who coined the terms extrovert and introvert, the difference between extroverts and introverts is the most important distinction between people because it indicates how their energy works.[5]

Privacy that requires solitude is not merely uncomfortable to extroverts; it also drains them. Introverts are the opposite; they may like other people, but interactions are draining, and they must pursue "solitary activities, working quietly alone, reading, meditating, participating in activities which involve few or no other people" in order to recover energy.[6]

Generally, introverts suffer more in daily life for they are outnumbered three to one and forced to conform to the standards of extroverts. However, extroverts suffer also as a result of common practices, in particular when privacy is offered as a perk or results from the isolation of high office. Otto Kroger and Janet Thuesen described a hypothetical administrator who, on reaching the top in his organization, is rewarded with a private office with a door normally closed. This, they said, shuts him off from the source of energy that has taken him to the top. Such a manager, they said, would establish an open-door policy and engage in "management by walking around."[7]

As a result of these differences in people, an increase in privacy will likely enhance the comfort and energy of introverts, while decreasing the same for extroverts. This will occur as long as the increase in privacy includes an increase in private spaces and solitary intervals. Increases in room-to-grow privacy are particularly hard on extroverts. Presumably, extroverts need such privacy in order to grow, but given a choice between growing or interacting, they often choose the latter. It is for this reason that some psychologists have noted that shallowness of personality is a danger of extreme extroversion.[8]

Of the four types of privacy under discussion here, room-to-grow privacy most strongly calls for isolation. But increases in the other kinds of privacy would probably also increase isolation noticeably for many extroverts. An increase in access-control privacy as it pertains to physical contact or observation by others would do so, as would an increase in safety-valve privacy, which might encourage some introverts to seek solitude rather than trusted groups, thereby reducing the size of groups on which extroverts have relied. An increase in respect privacy might reduce verbal intrusiveness and result in increased social distance.

A generalization can be made, then, that enhanced privacy works against extroverts, in particular by decreasing their energy; and if three out of four people are more extroverted than they are introverted, the decline in energy must be taken seriously. Enhanced privacy boosts a community's energy level only when people are more introverted than existing standards presume or when a community has grown more introverted while failing to adjust its customs accordingly.

Perhaps an awareness that privacy can be bad for extroverts motivates those who would limit privacy as a concept to access-control privacy involving information—in other words, to the right to limit the access of others to personal information about an individual. Access control is precisely the type of privacy that extroverts need and that does not threaten to increase the time they must spend alone. In short, it is the extrovert's brand of privacy.

Calls for greater privacy protection can, therefore, be broken down into two kinds: a call for the extrovert's brand—a narrow call that skirts the forms of privacy that prove to be pernicious for extroverts—and a call for the introvert's brand—a comprehensive call that would increase opportunities for private spaces, quiet moments, and solitary work.

Because most Americans are more extroverted than introverted, and endorse extroversion over introversion, one can surmise that the former call is more likely than the latter to succeed in the United States. A comparison of the United States to England casts different light on the possibilities, however. The English are so introverted by disposition that they have not needed specified moral or legal standards to protect privacy. The United States, then, appears to be a country in which a need for specified privacy protection has sprung from an inherent extroverted disposition—as an effort at self-correction. As a result, the call for comprehensive privacy protection might succeed to a minor degree, for the majority would support it out of a sense that it would be good for them, and the minority of introverts would certainly provide more enthusiastic support.

NOTES

1. Yehudi A. Cohen, *The Transition From Childhood to Adolescence* (Chicago: Aldine, 1964), p. 168.

2. Barrington Moore, Jr., *Privacy* (Armonk, NY: Sharpe, 1984), pp. 24–26.

3. David Keirsey and Marilyn Bates, *Please Understand Me* (Del Mar, CA: Prometheus Nemesis, 1984), p. 14.

4. Ibid., p. 14.

5. See Otto Kroger and Janet M. Thuesen, *Type Talk* (New York: Delacorte Press, 1988), p. 33.

6. Keirsey, *Please Understand Me*, p. 15.

7. Kroeger, *Type Talk*, p. 35.

8. Isabel Briggs Myers, *Gifts Differing* (Palo Alto, CA: Consulting Psychologists Press, 1980), p. 56.

Chapter 6

What Privacy Provides

George Steiner once said that "the present era in the West [is] one of a massive onslaught on human privacy."[1] Why did he see it this way? At first glance, the remark appears to be exaggerated, if not untrue. The remark came in an essay arguing that pornography was an assault on "the right to a private life of feeling."[2] As evidences of the massive onslaught, Steiner identified "urban mass technology, . . . uniformities of our economic and political choices, . . . electronic media, . . . sociological [and] psychological . . . intrusions and controls."[3] Otherwise, he did not elaborate. Steiner spoke for many who have not bothered to articulate their sense of loss. He gave a hint of his meaning in a note at the start of the 1967 publication of this essay: "Where everything can be said with a shout, less and less can be said in a low voice."[4]

Those who know what Steiner meant can feel it in their bones. Consider the result if you subject a person to some of the worst that the middle and late twentieth century has offered—if you subject a person to a regimen that includes the following in heavy doses:

a. Pornography;

b. Popular music at high volume, broadcast or recorded;

c. Psychological testing for security and hiring as well as for counseling and placement;

d. Heavy use of television and radio;

e. Pressure to disclose religious, political, and sexual thoughts to whomever asks;

f. Large crowds in home neighborhoods, schools, streets, workplaces, and public conveyances;

g. Examples of criminality among persons similar to one-self and among those one has considered emulating;

h. Treatment of the individual by governmental, educational, or job-related figures as a cipher interchangeable with other ciphers and without personal uniqueness;

i. Knowledge that your whereabouts, activities, habits, and finances are being tracked in governmental and commercial—and possibly mass media—files and computer data banks.

The result of such a regimen is a hardened person who is discouraged from listening to his or her own heart.

Steiner's 1967 essay was an attack on pornography only, but the author apparently took into consideration the potential cumulative impact of a variety of these twentieth-century affronts. While the cumulative impact of these affronts is potentially damaging, few people sustain the full damage possible. Yet many sustain partial damage, and Steiner knew this. He could safely guess that almost everyone dislikes the accumulation of privacy-destroying pressures, but it is likely that many do not know that life can be better in this respect, or that life, for at least a large plurality in America, was better in this regard until recently. What is more, many people do not believe that any improvements are possible and have devoted themselves to acquiring the hardness needed to live with the assaults.

In *Rabbit Redux*, John Updike gave his main character's prostitute sister an appropriate speech. The sister, Mim, in discussing her gangster boyfriends, says: "The men believe in flat stomach muscles and sweating things out. They don't want to carry too much fluid. You could say they're puritans. Gangsters are puritans. They're narrow and hard because of the straight path you don't live. . . . They're survival rules, rules for living in the desert." A little later she says, still referring to the gangsters: "Their one flaw is, they're still soft inside. They're like those chocolates we used to hate, those chocolate creams. . . . The other ones we hated, those dark brown round ones on the outside, all ooky inside. But that's how people are. It embarrasses everybody but they need to be milked. Men need to be drained. Like boils. Women too for that matter."[5]

Then Mim says, referring to the generation younger than her own: "[T]hat's what I do like about these kids: they're trying to kill it. Even if they kill themselves in the process." Her brother asks her, "Kill what?" She replies: "The softness. Sex, love; me, mine. They're doing it in. . . . They're burning it out with dope. They're going to make themselves hard clean through. Like, oh, cockroaches. That's the way to live in the desert. Be a cockroach. It's too late for you, and a little late for me, but once these kids get it together, they'll be no killing them. They'll live on poison."[6]

Whatever Updike was thinking when he wrote this—which must have been shortly after Steiner's article appeared—he was hitting close to Steiner's mark. In Steiner's terms, Updike's character's words were wrong in only a few respects; one, they were too bitter about the softness; two, they were false in suggesting that anyone happily adjusts to the hardness—although, in truth, Mim did not say anyone adjusted happily, only that she admired the adjustment of those younger than she was. She likened the conditions to which the young were adjusting to a desert, which is a useful symbol for a world without privacy, a desert being a climate that imposes maximum exposure without hope of shelter.

An environment that reduces privacy produces a hardened yet emptied person. Content that flourishes in quiet and in isolation is shouted, publicized, and scrutinized until it nearly ceases to exist. The resulting hardness of personality is not ordinary toughmindedness, ruthlessness, or competitiveness. The ambitions that drive ordinary hardness are, particularly at extremes, weaknesses—soft spots beneath the surface in which individuals define and know themselves yet which they seek to conceal in order to protect their vulnerability. Their self-esteem is low or they are ridden by fears, and they seek to compensate or overcompensate, adopting the mask of hardness to facilitate their striving; this is ordinary hardness. But the hardness that results from the accumulated deprivation of privacy is probably as characteristic of the non-competitive and self-effacing as it is of the aggressive. It is not a presence; it is an absence. Something is missing; "no one is home." The resulting personality is given to the implacable, machinelike completion of tasks in situations that call instead for the dropping of guises and the direct, flexible pursuit of values and of goals based on them.

It is not easy for a person to be "at home," inhabiting his or her own personality, when pressures tend to destroy this home. Thus it is important to guard the various types of privacy to ensure that there is an inhabitable home. When people have homes to inhabit, they more likely become the kinds of people we want—and need—and individually the people they want to be.

ETHICS

A code of ethics can be instilled without private moments, for example, by authority—beaten into a recruit. As a result, it may be unfair to suggest that the existence of ethical persons is based on privacy. However, privacy is crucial to ethics at several points. First, ethical systems are created or changed only by people who take time to ponder and introject about them. Second, no one makes ethical principles his or her own without mulling them over and modifying them into a personalized code. Third, one learns ethics faster who first masters the principles behind them and then moves on to the particulars; and it is in thoughtful isolation that a person masters basic principles.

It is difficult, then, to imagine a community of ethical people who are not also to some degree private people. Even if a community's ethics were perpetuated without privacy, community members would be thrust into privacy by their own violations of the code. Nothing generates moments of introspection faster than realizing that you have violated your own principles. The guilt, anxiety, or identity confusion that result from the violation will promptly cause self-examination.

Ethical standards, then, lead people into privacy even when the standards are created in environments that discourage privacy; however, these standards are usually the fruits of someone's solitary thought and usually are spread through thoughtful introspection by others.

SELF-CONTROL

Self-control is even more clearly based on privacy. It is an assertion by the private self. Self-control is not merely forbearance. Forbearance can be enforced externally by threats or by gentler or more clever compulsions. Self-control, by contrast, is forbearance from within, dictated by a point of consciousness that watches, waits, and regulates. This point of consciousness is private; it is what a person reserves to himself or herself in all interactions. It is the real person, no matter what social masks are displayed. Without this point of consciousness, a person is not a person; and if the point is not strong, the person has little self-control. As a result, self-control comes into existence when the inner point of consciousness is cultivated into a large private inner presence. This cannot happen unless time is taken to reflect alone and learn who one is. When you meet someone with self-control, you can be sure you are looking at a person who has had productive moments of privacy. A person with little self-control, by contrast, almost certainly is so enraptured by other people or so distracted by them, that he cannot stand his own company long enough to work out any sense of personal sovereignty.

Self-control is not a "nice" virtue; it has teeth in it. Self-control is often patience, and patience is often a strategy for winning. As a result, the private core of self that dictates control is often assertive or competitive, and it may even be ruthless. In some persons, the strategy of patience is almost unbeatable. As a result, in making self-control possible, privacy confers strength.

QUIET CERTAINTY

Quiet certainty, allowing a person to ignore crowd or peer pressure or to hear out an attacker without prematurely counterattacking, is probably seen most often in obviously private people. An obviously private person is more withdrawn in manner than the average person and contrives to spend as much time alone as he or she does with others. Of course, not all obviously private people are quietly certain, and some usually gregarious people prove to be quietly certain when pushed.

Quietly certain people occasionally make others angry. They dissent; they go their own way; they resist social pressures to which others succumb. They may do so calmly or irritably, with smiles or glares, but the message is the same: Such people have enviable independence.

They become this way in part because they are born this way, but also because they cultivate their separateness of judgment. Arguably, they would not cultivate such independence if they were not born with the tendency. Yet such people would not come into being if they had no room in which to cultivate their independence; and this room is privacy.

Privacy also permits such people to achieve certainty, which is the result of thought as well. Thought may take the form of logical analysis, careful reviewing of evidence, or patient searching for insights. But, like all thought, it does not occur unless other people leave the thinker alone. In truth, to say that certainty is generated by the kind of thought possible only in private is so obvious that it is embarrassing to have to say it. Yet, this understanding is so commonplace that it can easily be overlooked in evaluating the benefits of privacy. You simply do not find certainty as a trait except among people to whom privacy has been available.

REJECTION OF EXTRAVAGANCES AND IRREPRESSIBLE APPETITES

Is it possible that privacy could be behind the trait of reject-ing extravagance and overcoming irrepressible appetites? The answer is yes, but only in part. Privacy thwarts the impulse to extravagance because it directs attention to the inner life.[7] Al-though in large doses it isolates a person, in more reasonable doses it merely adds depth, curing superficiality. A person of-fered private moments, who has a will to exploit these mo-ments, at least senses that enduring values cannot be met with material goods no matter how high the quality. Such a person will not feel that he or she must have it all—or show it all. The traits that provoke a person to master appetites are a drive to avoid enslavement to anything, plus a commitment to patience as a personal style and life strategy. Moments spent in private enhance one's sense of personal integrity. You get to know you are special, and you do not want to throw away yourself. Con-trol of appetites follows as a sword and shield. Also, if you take yourself seriously enough to regard your pleasures as valid and self-enhancing, you do not want to discard the prospect of years of satisfaction merely for a risky short-term indulgence. A per-son who makes good use of available privacy is freer from wants and urges and is rewarded with greater satisfaction of some of these same appetites.

ABSENCE OF DEEP INSECURITIES AND FEARS

Few virtues exceed in importance that of being free of deep insecurities or fears. This is a social virtue as well as a personal one because people pained by their own insecurities or fears cause pain. Behind every ugly personality is a hidden self pre-occupied with terror or self-disgust. How does one root out original suffering like this in order to give a person some inner tranquillity and other people a break?

The most fearful or self-disgust-ridden people might argue that the best strategy for them is to avoid private moments as often as possible. Their rationale is that a whirl of extroverted activity distracts the sufferer and reduces the occasions in which he cannot escape from himself. The defect in this strategy is that the terrible messages are always there within, always known, and always waiting. As a result, they influence the very behaviors chosen as escapes, perverting them, frustrating them, and leading the person to the double dissatisfaction that comes when the social whirl aborts, enemies are made instead of friends, love is unrequited, guilt surges as a consequence of exploiting others, acquaintances grow chilly, and the sufferer is left alone.

A private confrontation with the fears or self-disgust often cannot be escaped unless the person dies during the flight. By the time the flight ends, either in death or in the reckoning, at least a few other people have been hurt as the sufferer has expressed his or her pain and spread it around. How much better it is to move more directly to the work that only privacy allows: addressing the fears or replacing the self-disgust with an endorsement of one's virtues.

Everyone has fears and insecurities; no one learns to manage them without privacy. This is so even when the person seeks help, either in formal counseling or through the services of a friend. Help sends the person back to the private confrontation with himself or herself, with momentum and guidance, but without company. The cure or the healing insight requires privacy. Even if it does not arrive in a private moment, the individual must take a private moment to absorb it, possibly a long private interlude. The arrival of the insight breaks into the person's then current extroverted involvement; individuals who have not learned to value privacy may not be willing to pull away from extroverted engagements and may lose their insights.

EMOTIONAL CONTROL

Emotional control is not considered to be a virtue by everyone. The words suggest a stiff upper lip and an English insistence on coolness. A body of argument in psychology suggests that it is healthier to express emotions. To a degree, the issue is politicized, women sometimes criticizing men for being unexpressive emotionally. Emotional control is not synonymous with emotional restraint. A Latin or Russian temper can result from emotional virtuosity, from skilled and controlled expression of emotion. Emotional control is compatible with considerable emotional expression. Viewed this way, emotional control may appeal to—or may be recognized by—a wider variety of people.

Do privacy-oriented people lack emotional control? Not usually. Do they experience great emotionality? Yes; in particular, the still-waters-run-deep type does.

Emotional control differs from self-control in that the former is control of expression while the latter is control of appetites. Yet, control is control, and the existence of control indicates the presence of a controller. As a result, we are returned to the point of consciousness at the core of a personality, the point that, when amplified, gives a person possession of himself or herself. As argued above, moments of privacy allow one to enhance this core in order to achieve self- control. If people have not developed control, they might find themselves with only two choices regarding their emotions: to suppress them or to unleash them. Only by extending control to the emotions can persons increase their choices and hope to reach a condition in which they can direct their emotional expression as they would one of their limbs.

Such control is based on knowledge of one's emotions and of one's priorities as to what one feels should be expressed, and on practice in the expression. The last is not something done in solitude; emotional practice might include intimate exchanges with important others, but it is not private in the sense that the former two are. Knowledge of one's emotions results from testing them in the cauldron of interaction and reflecting on them afterwards. Establishing priorities as to what one feels should be expressed requires erecting a hierarchy of values, and this work requires solitude and reflection. In fact, it requires an element of meditation; the gut component is perhaps more important than the cerebral one. As a result, the development of emotional control requires withdrawal and return, testing and reflection; private moments are an important part of this.

Some persons can avoid developing their own emotional control by adopting conventional manners of expression, and these conventional manners might get them through most emotional challenges. Such people would not have to employ privacy in developing their emotional expression, but their ways of expressing themselves might strike sensitive others as inauthentic.

Did the present eras bring an onslaught against privacy, as Steiner claimed? One way to make this judgment is to consider whether any of the personal traits that privacy fosters became less evident after the middle of the twentieth century. If the traits declined, this might indicate that privacy declined also. In sum, the traits did decline; therefore, Steiner was at least partially correct.

Some of these traits are obviously in decline. Firm ethics, self-control, quiet certainty, restraint in consumption and appetites, and emotional control have all grown less important as values. Of course, substantial numbers of people dedicate themselves to recovering these values. For example, evangelical Christians pursue them through their churches, and drug and alcohol counselors pursue them through public campaigns calling for restraint. But these are reactions to a trend running the other way, toward situational ethics, loss of self-control, personal uncertainty, compulsive over-indulgence, and emotional profligacy.

In the area of ethics, cleverness-makes-right has become an attractive alternative to consistent ethics, even among law-abiding people. Money matters appear to have encouraged this change. Devotion to the bottom line is not an approach that encourages ethicality. The frequent discovery of corruption in high places paradoxically signals not that society does not tolerate corruption, but that everyone is corrupt and only a few are caught. Weakness in the economy, the decline in real income, the shrinkage of the middle class, the advance of income inequality, and the extension of celebrity status to the very wealthy may have increased the average person's ruthlessness in economic matters. However, the trend may have little to do with economic pressure. It may have resulted because many no longer take the time to develop ethical codes and therefore find themselves empty-handed in ethical crises.

Situational ethics is a progressive concept when it refers to replacing ethical rigidity with flexibility. Every situation is unique, and formulaic approaches can be heartless. Yet situational ethics are too often excuses for the absence of any ethics at all. It is never ethical for a reporter to make up a fact in order to round out a touching news story, or for a professor to give a better grade to the more obnoxious of two nearly equal students simply because the more obnoxious one is more likely to ruin the professor's day. It is never ethical for a psychiatrist to have sex with a patient, no matter how legitimate is his belief that the patient is needy, or for a job applicant to falsify his or her credentials. It is not ethical for a student to cheat on a test, even if he legitimately hates the instructor, or for a man to rape a woman who is so drunk she does not know the difference, even though she should have known better than to drink heavily in rowdy company. It is not ethical to use a herbicide that you believe is dangerous to health when you live in a crowded neighborhood, even though you desperately want your shrubs to grow and are willing to risk your own health. It is not ethical to leave a board with nails in it or a broken bottle on a road when you can easily lift or kick it aside, even though you are sure someone else will remove it. Nevertheless, some of these behaviors became more or less acceptable—maybe not quite right, but understandable and excusable—under the standard of situational ethics.

Few Americans in the late twentieth century would be surprised if culprits such as those committing the activities described above faced formal censure for violating an organizational or professional code, as might a student caught cheating or a psychiatrist discovered to have slept with a patient. But many people would not personally condemn the culprits, would not regard them as diminished as persons by their actions. In fact, the actors might freely disclose these acts to close friends without guilt or fear of criticism. In other words, many people would regard these transgressions as we all regard traffic violations. A person ticketed for speeding 10 miles per hour over the limit, failing to observe a stop sign, or driving out of lane might admit guilt and pay a fine, but no one will regard the person as ethically flawed or personally diminished. Many people view true ethical transgressions similarly, believing that these occur only when one is caught, and that even then they have only formal or impersonal significance. A person might have to answer when he violates an organizational code, but he is not expected to follow a personal one.

In this sense, people generally may have become less ethical than they have once been. Many people have no investment in personal ethics; and, as a result, they lack something that privacy provides.

In the area of self-control, impatience has, for many, replaced the controlled, dogged pursuit of objectives. This shows up in the job planning of college students, many of whom unreasonably expect high salaries early in their careers, and some of whom abandon aspirations as soon as they learn that high pay is not quickly available in the work that they preferred. In short, they do not take their personal uniqueness seriously when they plan their work lives and do not have a sense of being sovereign individuals dedicated to realizing their uniqueness in the worlds of economics or service. Instead, they appear to be ready to relinquish what sense of themselves they have in order to earn large sums of money fast. Some may define themselves as persons devoted to money, with money being a symbol of power, responsibility, or influence. But for most, money represents only what it can buy; and the insistence on a high salary early in a career is an insistence on high early consumption. This is a strategy of individuals who find personal identity not in work, service, or action in or upon the world, but instead in patterns of consumption.

The element of self-control is so different in such people from what it has been in others, that it is no longer the kind of control that privacy fosters. Such people, for example, can easily be controlled or bullied. They can be controlled though the offering of money or of luxuries: cars, clothes, liquors, vacations, mail-order steaks, houses, furniture. For people who define themselves by what they consume, there is no shame in being bought; instead, for them, to be bought is to be successful, provided the goods, the creature comforts they impart, and the status they provide are of adequate quality. Such people can be bullied by the threat of depriving them of the same. They do not insist on personal sovereignty because they do not value it.

As a result, consumption-oriented people in a consumer society need little of what privacy offers. What they want is quick satisfaction of appetites; a concern for personal sovereignty interferes with satiating such appetites. In the late twentieth century, the wealthiest countries have become consumer societies to a degree, and some people in them have responded by resting their identities on their patterns of consumption. As a result, they have found less use for some traits that privacy builds. While this change may not amount to an onslaught against privacy, it has reduced somewhat the importance of privacy to personal development.

While quiet certainty may have declined in the later twentieth century, it is difficult to document this change. Large numbers of people have become lost—do not know what they want from life, cannot choose a mate or trust themselves to choose one, have no philosophy of life, and cannot invest themselves in the lives they are living. Also, numbers are large of people who must have the endorsement of others even in small matters— who do not know whether what they say is right until someone else approves, who do not know what is important until someone else responds, who do not know what is beautiful or ugly until someone else agrees. It is hard to know your own mind when herd participation and peer pressure are the dominating experiences of youth and young adulthood. Development of quiet certainty seems unimportant when the strongest drive experienced is to achieve recognized position and popularity.

Quiet certainty allows a person to go it alone. But to many, being alone has no value under any circumstances; and to the extent that the numbers of such people have increased, quiet certainty has declined.

Restraint regarding consumption and appetites has clearly declined. This change has appeared most troublingly in heavy drug use. It also appears in buying habits. The hunger for power has begun to look like an untamed appetite.

According to a Confucian axiom, to live a balanced and productive life, one must avoid three hazards, each of which is characteristic of a stage of life. Lust is the hazard of the young. The desire for power is the hazard of the middle aged. Greed is the hazard of the old. This Confucian rule is too austere for Americans, but there is wisdom in it. As the twentieth century ends, some Americans appear to have inverted the injunctions into an endorsement of lust, hunger for power, and material accumulation. This is particularly true if drug lust is counted as a form of lust. The drugs of choice in this era are not sexual depressors—the opiates—but instead drugs, such as cocaine, amphetamines, and derivatives that are reported to have one or more sexualizing effects. These popular drugs, then, have at least some remote sexual connection, which brings them onto the periphery of lust even if we give lust its traditional definition as sexual exploitation. Drug use characterizes our times, for many Americans at many different levels of society use drugs heavily. That they do so is a sign that many are dominated by their appetites.

At the same time, extravagance appears to be growing. During the 1980s it became acceptable to show rather than hide wealth. "Upscale" marketing emerged as a trend, fed by the growth of upper middle-class incomes as the rest of the middle class struggled with less and the lower class slipped toward poverty. Cars five to six times as costly as the average car were purchased in large enough numbers that they clearly were no longer only the toys of hidden aristocrats. A similar process occurred with respect to clothing, furnishings, jewelry, and vacations. Extravagance returned.

The ability to say no to extravagance or to other appetites is a strength that privacy affords; but this ability has less importance in the late twentieth-century world than it did just a few decades ago.

Emotional control appears not to have noticeably declined. Some emotional rampancy has always been evident in the

United States. The Jim Crow policies of the late nineteenth century through the mid-twentieth century were fueled by a wild paranoia as well as a nostalgia. The fear that whites had of blacks and the angry dreams they had of the "good old days" when blacks knew their places overtook their intelligence. As the twenty-first century approaches, racial affairs involving blacks and whites remain emotional on both sides, with the only difference being that the percentage of whites lost to emotionality has probably declined. Regarding communism, American emotional control increased from the mid-twentieth century. The dark terror of communism characteristic of the 1950s had all but disappeared by 1990. The reason for this change was a decline in communism as a force in the world, a decline rashly interpreted by many Americans as a victory of American capitalism over Soviet communism. In fact, American capitalism was in trouble at the time. The change in the American attitude amounted, however, to achievement of a new emotional control among Americans regarding the Soviet Union and other communist countries, a new control that was rewarded with the collapse of the Union of Soviet Socialist Republics and the near death of international communism. The United States was at the time losing ground in non-ideological economic wars with Japan, East Asia, and the European Economic Community, but America's imminent loss of global economic primacy has yet to spawn reckless emotionality in Americans. Currently Americans have not lost ground—and possibly have gained—in emotional control regarding the two major fears of the preceding century: other races and communism.

By contrast, exhibitions of low emotional control probably have become more commonplace in everyday life. The principle that the squeaky wheel gets the oil appears to have gained acceptance as a justification for obnoxious behavior in staking out claims to limited resources. Emotional control is no longer expected of school children, including high school children; their outbursts are often taken as the soul cries of victims and excused, maybe even encouraged, at least up to the point where others are subjected to battery. Similar tolerance has extended to more mature persons. For example, college students are not expected to behave quite as though adult and therefore are not taken to task for failing to do so.

Adults belonging to a variety of victimized or underprivileged groups are permitted outbursts in which emotions swamp intelligence. This dispensation has extended to members of minority groups, women, foreigners, and the poor. By 1990, it was also being extended to groups of white men when they were isolated or under attack. The privilege has extended to society's victims and to members of any aggregate that can be called an ethnic minority. The privilege is not consistently exercised, but it has been used. Honoring the privilege, few listeners would challenge the speaker or think less of him or her as a result of an outburst, although some listeners might thereafter avoid the speaker when possible, the toleration for verbal abuse as an experience not having kept pace with the toleration for it in principle.

In other ways, the demand for emotional control has evaporated. Bus drivers and cab drivers, for example, are no longer expected to be courteous. The same is true of some others whose work requires them to meet the public: some civil service office workers, some garbage men, some meter readers, some delivery persons, even some flight attendants. One can even find the same freedom to be unpleasant when exercised by school staff and faculty, fast-food workers, secretaries, hospital workers, mechanics, professors, police officers, lawyers. The decline in emotional control amounts to a decline in civility. The rule that one should keep one's inner turmoil to oneself appears to have been retired and replaced with a new rule that allows people to inflict their emotional pain on others, or even to take it out on others to a degree that stops short of wild shouting or threats of blows. A country that has been characterized by limited civility is becoming one of abrasive and crabby people.

The spread of routine unpleasantness and the loss of any expectation that people might behave otherwise provides the strongest evidence that emotional control had declined. Are people called upon to keep their emotional unreasonableness to themselves? No—not if they belong to a group commonly regarded as victimized; not if they are considered less than fully grown; not if they are appealing for a share of limited resources; and not if they restrict themselves to crabbiness, cattiness, obnoxiousness, abrasiveness, depressiveness, or maudlinism without slipping beyond into threats of violence, shouting, or sobbing. Yet, if emotional control has declined, the decline is not decisive enough to justify a claim that an onslaught has occurred in this area of privacy.

Although some people might view the reduction of privacy hopefully, interpreting it to be part of the emergence of a new model of character or a new value system, the change has occurred as the United States weakened and has to be considered against this background.

Richard Barnet wrote the following in the January 1, 1990 edition of *The New Yorker*, in an article entitled "After the Cold War":

> The highly publicized failures of socialism in undeveloped countries and the extraordinary prosperity within the United States in recent years make the idea of an American perestroika seem preposterous. Yet the United States is squandering capital to maintain an ephemeral prosperity that is politically unstable, because it is based on increasing inequality. Consider the cumulative consequences of the conditions which the United States finds itself facing: a unique dependence on foreign financing of its debt; the paucity of long-term investment in industrial production, the modernization of services, or public infrastructure; the lack of a coherent policy on technological development, which puts the country at a serious competitive disadvantage; a frenzied, "get rich quick" economy, in the grip of takeovers, leveraged buyouts, and other manifestations of what Keynes called the "casino" economy; the descent into poverty of almost a fifth of the nation's children; the growing disparity between cities and regions with rising prospects and the large areas of the nation that are being abandoned by both government and industry; and a seeming inability to re-

duce significantly a military establishment much of which is increasingly irrelevant to real security needs. Still used to thinking of ourselves as "the No. 1 nation," as President Lyndon Johnson did twenty-one years ago, the people of the United States have actually fallen behind the people in other leading industrial countries with respect to maternal health, literacy, infant mortality, drug dependence, and education. We are five percent of the world's population, and it appears that we consume more than half of the hard drugs on the global market. By these crucial measures, the security of the United States is eroding.[8]

If Barnet's list is accurate, something unfortunate has happened. Arguably this deterioration is related to the loss of privacy, or of the traits privacy nurtures: self-control, which encourages planning; quiet certainty, which gives resistance to peer pressure and vogues; and restraint, which curbs greed and appetites. What privacy fosters the country appears to need; what it discourages the country apparently needs to be without.

NOTES

1. George Steiner, "Night Words," in George Steiner, *Language and Silence* (New York: Atheneum, 1967), p. 74.
2. Ibid.
3. Ibid. The whole passage reads:

Future historians may come to characterize the present era in the West as one of a massive onslaught on human privacy, on the delicate processes by which we seek to become our own singular selves, to hear the echo of our specific being. This onslaught is being pressed by the very conditions of an urban mass-technology, by the necessary uniformities of our economic and political choices, by the new electronic media of communications and persuasion, by the ever-increasing exposure of our thoughts and actions to sociological, psychological, and material intrusions and controls. Increasingly, we come to know real privacy, real space in which to experiment with our sensibilities only in extreme guises, nervous breakdown, addiction, economic failure.

4. Ibid., p. 68.

5. John Updike, *Rabbit Redux* (New York: Knopf, 1971), pp. 359–360.

6. Ibid., p. 361.

7. According to the Myers-Briggs theory of personality types, the persons least inclined toward extravagance are introverts and, in particular, introverts strong in logical thought and judgmental in their approaches to external pressures on them. The least extravagance oriented of any type of person, according to the theory, is the type described as an ISTJ, an introverted, sensing, thinking, judgmental person. Such people are attuned to concrete evidence and sensory enjoyment and take a logical, judgmental approach to routine problems. This type is also described as the most private of the sixteen types identified in the theoretical framework, even though such people are said to usually involve themselves significantly in community service. A type described in the Myers-Briggs theory as ESFP appears to be the most inclined toward extravagance, at least to extravagance defined as creature comforts that conform to prevailing fashions. This type is the extroverted, sensing, feeling, perceptual kind of person. These people are keen about sensory experience, non-judgmental in dealing with worldly matters, and feeling oriented in their inner lives. Such people are not private and dislike being alone. Their dislike of solitary moments and their susceptibility to pleasant distractions often frustrates their academic efforts—the academy relying on study, and study requiring privacy.

As a result, the life patterns of the ESFP person and the ISTJ person reveal an inverse relationship between extravagance and privacy. Private people, then, naturally reject extravagance, while non-private people who are extravagant can moderate their extravagance by cultivating a taste for privacy. Similarly, the highly private ISTJ is usually matter-of-fact, even about appetites, and orderly in satisfying them. The non-private ESFP is, by contrast, vulnerable to being swept away by surges of sensation or feeling and to have more difficulty saying no. The Myers-Briggs theory, then, suggests an inverse relationship between privacy and irrepressible appetites.

It would be false and meanspirited to assert that ISTJ personalities are better than ESFP personalities. Also, such a suggestion would offend an objective of the Myers-Briggs theory, which is to promote tolerance of others. Both ISTJ and ESFP types of people have flaws and virtues. In addition, an unbalanced ISTJ might fall captive to undeveloped, previously unexpressed sides of his or her own personality and plunge into extravagance or uncontrolled appetites far more recklessly than a matured ESFP would. But freedom from showing off, over-spending, or over-indulging is by definition a virtue of one of these types, while enslavement to the same is a risk for the other. See Isabel Briggs Myers, *Gifts Differing* (Palo Alto, CA: Consulting Psychologists Press, 1980).

8. Richard J. Barnet, "After the Cold War," *The New Yorker* 65, no. 46 (January 1, 1990); 75.

_____ Chapter 7 _____

Sexual Assault

Rape is a crime emblematic of an invasion of privacy. All kinds of sexual assaults are invasions of privacy, as are the subtle assaults known collectively as sexual harassment. In the United States near the end of the twentieth century, the growing intolerance toward sexual assault and sexual harassment is a sign that privacy is generally appreciated more than it has been.

Although rapes and sexual harassment appear to have been increasing in incidence since the 1970s, statistics do not reveal whether there has been an actual increase or whether the frequency of reporting has simply increased.[1]

Also increasing since the 1980s, and clearly so, is the American public's sense of outrage at these crimes. The outrage regarding rape is traceable in part to the insistence by feminists and other outspoken women that rape is indeed outrageous. It is also linked to the increase in the incidence or reporting of rape, which gives men and women the impression that they are surrounded by episodes of rape. Many people have come to understand that rape clearly is not something that happens only rarely and then only to women who ask for it. On the contrary, it is a daily occurrence.

The traditional response of women to news of rape was to conclude that men were rotten and not to be trusted. The traditional response of male friends and family of a female rape victim was to seek out and kill the rapist. These old attitudes began to coalesce during the 1980s in an increased willingness to prosecute alleged rapists. Problems of proof have remained, however, and will always remain, and because the charge is serious, jurors appeared to automatically take with equal seriousness the proof standards meant to protect the innocent.

The outrage regarding rape is traceable to a widely shared, heightened recognition that privacy is important—that it matters that someone is raped, that everyone is somehow affected, that an environment that tolerates rape will also tolerate a range of invasions of one's own privacy.

The desire to assert power has always been an incentive to invade privacy, though it is not the only incentive. Sometimes invasions have resulted from accidents, ignorance, or the simple need for information. But often the motive for invading privacy is to exert power over the person whose privacy is invaded. This is a motive to not merely control another person's behavior but to also break his or her heart or spirit so that one's domination can approach completeness. The invasions used to achieve a result of domination often have been sexual. Homosexual prison rapes clearly have this motive. So did rapes of slave women by slave masters or their employees in all of the many countries that have permitted slavery to exist. In these instances the rapes—and the quid pro quo harassment by powerful figures in the slave systems—invaded not only the privacy of the women targeted but also the privacy of their families. It kept the underlings broken. The exercise of the first night right by feudal masters had a similar effect. The invasion of privacy, the abuse of power, and unwanted sex have had a long and ugly history of association. As a result, when Americans looked at sexual assault and harassment in 1990, they saw bullies at work, satisfying a lust for power by invading privacy; many found the images to be unacceptable.

One reason the invasion of privacy has garnered attention during the second half of the twentieth century is that many people realize that it is an abuse of power. It is close-up bullying that we reject when we reject an invasion of privacy. It is a right to be respectable within ourselves and inviolate that we assert when we demand that our privacy be respected. Nothing comes closer to symbolizing the problem than rape does.

As the 1990s began, rape was still being classified in public discussion as a crime not of sex but of violence. The purpose of the classification was to emphasize that rapes did not occur simply because a man was sexually attracted to or aroused by a woman—something the woman might be able to control— but for other reasons attributable strictly to the man. But the classification was misleading because sex was part of the crime. Rape is a crime of sex, violence, power, and an invasion of privacy. In a rape, power is asserted by invading privacy through sexual means with violence employed or threatened. All elements are there together.[2]

The feeling of having been soiled is characteristic not only of having suffered rape, but also of having been subjected to any of a wide variety of other invasions of privacy. The feeling may be almost disabling in intensity for some sexual assault victims, but even fairly innocuous conversational invasions of privacy— as by meddlesome persons or those who seek a kind of intimacy by making ugly personal disclosures—leave a listener feeling soiled. In fact, if you find yourself wanting to take a shower after a conversation, you can be almost certain that someone has just invaded your privacy.[3]

A rapist's objective is to break his victim. Sometimes this is an act of gratuitous self-aggrandizement. Sometimes it is an act of general anger, as against all women. Sometimes it is anger at a particular woman, who is perceived as someone who must be knocked down. Sometimes it is an act by a man who can overcome his fear of women only through a gross strategy of domination. Sometimes it is action by ignorant and unempathic men who have believed myths that women are different from men in actually preferring to be broken. Infrequently women rape other women, using found objects for penetration, in acts of domination or of expressing anger through domination. Sometimes men rape other men, as in the efforts of prison inmates to make slaves of other prisoners. Sometimes women have managed to rape men or boys, to show them who is boss.

As the 1990s began, many people had caught on that no one wants to be broken and that even the unbreakable do not want anyone to try to dominate them. As a result, a constituency developed to prevent actions that could break people by invading their privacy.

Sexual harassment continued to present problems of definition in the early 1990s and served as a reminder that not all invasions of privacy can be remedied. Incidents of sexual harassment are problematical except at the extremes. They present a vast gray area, and in this gray area subtle factors determine whether a behavior is harassment. The evidentiary difficulties are great; it is better when cases are heard before witnesses start to lose a fresh and rich memory of these subtle factors.[4] Due to these subtleties, much that is experienced as sexual harassment cannot be penalized as sexual harassment: the tenth request for a date, according to the recipient, which, according to the requester, is merely a collegial suggestion that they have lunch together; the comment about a woman's buttocks, according to the woman, which the commenter says was a compliment on the fit of a new pair of slacks; the arm around the waist that the recipient says was presumptuous and intimate, but which the owner of the arm says was a natural gesture between two people who dated in the past and are currently unattached; a touch to the face that the recipient calls an erotic liberty but which, according to the toucher, was acceptably spontaneous because sparks had flown between the two even if the recipient had ambivalent feelings.

Much alleged harassment is verbal and raises free speech problems. The speech right in the American tradition, popular and legal, even among those who do not regard free speech as an absolute right, cannot be curbed without strong justification. The justification of protecting workers from sabotage to their performance in the workplace—an equal opportunity justification usually cited as a foundation for sexual harassment regulations—does not apply once workers leave the work site; and if it is applied so strictly in the workplace as to extinguish all opportunities for romance among workers, it will lose the support of those whom it has been designed to protect, and eventually it will be honored principally in the breach. It is not difficult to imagine a time when many men and some women may regard the filing of sexual harassment complaints against them as status-enhancing "red badges of courage."

The sexual harassment case in which a superior has promised a promotion in return for sexual favors and has been overheard by a third party doing so, or in which one person has actually fondled another in a supply closet or elevator, is a relief for those charged with enforcing harassment regulations. Only the extreme cases are easy.

Sexual harassment becomes more understandable when it is recognized as an invasion of privacy. Efforts to curb sexual harassment are not efforts to curb sex, but to curb invasions of privacy; and recognition that an invasion of privacy is at the bottom of an incident of sexual harassment is a reminder that sex and sexual harassment are not identical.

Many women view sexual harassment as an issue of workplace power. Men who harass in the workplace, they say, are motivated by a desire to hold off a challenge by women as competing co-workers and, as a result, employ harassments to block women's advancement. This view has been adopted in rationales supporting anti-sexual harassment regulations as equal opportunity measures.

This view may represent an accurate reading of a few men, but, on the whole, it is misleading. Most male sexual harassers are not motivated by power-ladder considerations. The legal theory that harassment is an equal opportunity issue is a legal fiction, as far as male motivations are concerned. Most male harassers, like most female ones, are motivated by sex. They are willing to use power to gain a sexual advantage, but they are not motivated to use sex to gain a power advantage.

In the vast gray area of possibly inappropriate comments, many remarks although sexual in inspiration are not sexual harassment, in that they are driven by no intent to invade and in impact do not invade. The man who repeatedly asks a woman out even though he receives "no" each time, is motivated by a sexual interest in the woman plus a persistent temperament. His flaw is that he does not have enough self-consciousness to recognize when his persistence becomes a nuisance. All too soon it becomes de facto harassment.

The man who regularly makes comments on a woman's appearance—such as complimenting her on her attire—finds the woman attractive, has no hope or intention of establishing any intimate bond with her, and seeks to make a few daily flatterings serve as substitutes for all that cannot be; in short, he engages in pure flirting. Doing so is alright when it is appreciated for what it is or when it is part of happy but inconsequential exchanges; but when the woman finds it to be offensive—as when she is introverted, or truly not playful, or finds the man repulsive, or simply does not like people talking about her body, or is powerfully affected and flustered by the flattery—then the comments invade her privacy and amount to harassment. How does a man know when to stop? When he senses she does not like it or when she asks him to stop, it is time for him to stop. This is not a situation easy to handle in formal proceedings under a sexual harassment complaint.

The man who occasionally makes comments on a woman's appearance may be motivated by a genuine, abstracted appreciation with no sense of sexual interest at all—as might be true of a man who has daughters and has acquired the habit of complimenting them. But a man who makes occasional comments might, on the other hand, be totally false, making the comments methodically, without any real appreciation at all, because he is convinced that women should be, and like to be, complimented occasionally. Such a man may compliment women who do not look good to him in any way. Yet, some women might object to his comments; and if he persists in making them, he will be invading their privacy, even though he would be perfectly happy not to comment at all.

Comments that call attention to the fact that the sexes are different, or that imply a difference between the sexes, or that cause a woman to be momentarily self-conscious that she is a woman in the presence of men, or that cause a man to become similarly self-conscious among women are offensive to those who under some circumstances want to forget that there are sexes. So, they call these comments sexual harassment. People who like to think there are no significant differences between the sexes, who see the sexes as minor variations on a single theme, rarely make remarks that can be challenged as sexual harassments. Those who, on the contrary, like to think that sexual differences are fundamental, that people enjoy belonging to their sexes, and that people are happier when their sexual identity is acknowledged often make remarks that can be challenged as sexual harassment. The former follow an androgynous model. The latter follow a differentiated model. Vast numbers of persons subscribe to each model and react to remarks of sexual recognition in vastly different ways. What strikes an androgynous person to the quick, invading his or her privacy and constituting harassment, might bring to a differentiated person joy, shining like sunlight through clouds to make that person's day. A great difficulty in addressing sexual harassment, then, is to prevent invasions of the androgynous while keeping the sun shining for the differentiated. The only way to manage this difficulty effectively is to insist upon sensitivity to the subjective experiences of invasion that others might have, while requiring that those experiencing invasion offer some signal that they find comments or actions to be offensive. Sexual harassment in the gray area will never be easy to distinguish or penalize.

Some men do seek a competitive advantage over women by using sexual harassment to rattle them. Women do the same to men, and in a sense women have an easier time of it because men are more quickly aroused. Thus a woman might be able to fluster a man by provoking a sexual sensation in him at an inappropriate time. Men try to fluster women less with the intent of actually cuing sexual reactions in women than by startling them with their willingness to invade. Such sallies by men or women have little impact on the kind of recipients who become quickly angered, but they may take a toll on those who do not become angry but simply become confused. Such uses of sexual harassment do present an equal protection problem or an unfair competition problem because their intent is a power advantage. However, even when a power motivation is absent, comments that androgynous persons find invasive will be experienced by them as thwarting them in their performance of job tasks; and, as a result, they will be ready to attribute a power motive to the comments. In other words, such comments to a follower of the androgynous model create a competitive disadvantage as an effect no matter what the intent, such is the level of sensitivity in some people.

Sensitivity to individuals and giving others a veto is the key to effective etiquette in the workplace. In this respect, sexual harassment resembles date rape, in which willingness to take "no" for an answer cures the problem.

Date rape—or acquaintance rape—is not merely sexual harassment of a higher degree; it is sex, not words; it is real action, not verbal action. Many people will argue that words can hurt, as indeed they can. Yet a society that values freedom of speech, self-restraint, and tolerance lives by the distinction. The distinction between words and actions is deeply rooted in American customs.[5] It means that rapes of any kind are qualitatively different from sexual harassment. The invasions of privacy that constitute sexual harassment must be balanced against constitutional guidelines and other traditions defending speech; but those invasions that make up rape are invasions of privacy pure and simple and do not have to be balanced against other values.

Acquaintance rape is a man's taking advantage of a woman who trusted him by forcing her to submit to sexual acts. Acquaintance rape includes a variety of offenses ranging from the rape of girls by family friends to surprise assaults of women in non-sexual settings. As of 1990, acquaintance rape was most commonly understood in the United States to be forced sexual intercourse taking place in a setting defined at least in part as sexual or romantic, such as a man and woman on a date or drinking together in a party environment. Hence, "date rape" became the more commonly used term. The typical image invoked by the term "date rape" is of a couple alone in a room after an outing, sharing a drink and engaging in light sexual play, maybe even heavy sexual play, the man moving toward sexual intercourse, the woman resisting and saying no because she never intended to have intercourse, and the man overpowering her.

Apparently since 1990, date rape has been common, in particular on college campuses.[6] Although much can be said to distinguish the motivations of one date rapist from another, and although women can be criticized for being so stupid as to put themselves in vulnerable situations, the underlying fact of date rapes is that they are indeed rapes because the parties are not in agreement. Agreement may exist even though neither party says a word, but if the woman says no or physically struggles to escape an embrace, agreement does not exist and sexual intercourse or any sexual intensification of the encounter violates the woman's privacy. If, on the other hand, the woman is ambivalent but has intercourse and then feels used afterward, this is not an invasion of privacy or rape; it is a bad decision by the woman, and the fact that she made it in a split, overheated second does not convert the event into a crime against her. Unfortunately, by the early 1990s the definition of date rape had become so loose that sometimes it was applied to situations in which the woman agreed to have sex but afterward wished she had not and also wished that the man had not been so pushy. This was not rape; and calling it rape mocked the concept so badly that public faith in anti-rape efforts was weakened and the new tide of needed prosecutions jeopardized, at just the time when the increasing appreciation of privacy had evoked in many persons a refusal to tolerate real rapes.[7] On the other hand, a man's engaging in sex with a woman who is too drunk or too drugged to perceive what is happening is rape.

Many date rapists apparently are not premeditative rapists. Instead, many appear to be simply men who cannot clearly perceive women's signals as to when to start and stop, simply because it seems to them that some women say "no" only perfunctorily, or intend "yes" even as they say "no," or say "no" only because they are ambivalent but are leaning toward saying "yes." In fact, date rape has captured the imagination of many as being a signaling problem among ordinary daters, and publicity campaigns have been launched—for example, on college campuses—to stress the theme that "when she says 'no,' she means 'no.' "

It had been clear for decades, and probably for centuries, that "when she says 'no,' she means 'no' "; in fact, it was because of this understanding that generation after generation of college men applied themselves strenuously to the business of convincing her to say "yes." As a result, if indeed, as of the 1990s large numbers of young men no longer sought to convince her, but instead simply barged ahead when her resistance affronted their sense of urgency, then some mutation in understanding had occurred.

If large numbers of men are behaving in this way, one must ask why. After all, it is otherwise ordinary young men who engage in date rape, not men who can experience sexual arousal only when they are violent—people who have to rape to have any sex at all—but simply men who are comfortable with bullying weaker people to take what they want. If this is what they are—sexually conventional but inclined to bully—then date rape as a crime has begun to occupy a niche previously monopolized by armed robbery. It has become a second litmus test to measure the depth of true criminality in a community. Homicide, other than that committed during a robbery, is not a measure of true criminality for it results from passions, pains, fears, desperation, and despair over the value of human life. But armed robbery, and now perhaps also date rape, are measures of the willingness to simply take what the taker wants—without regard to the needs, rights, or privacy of others.

Some date rapists are in a separate category—the premeditative rapists for whom date rape is a mentally challenging alternative to stranger rape. In 1991, the prosecutor in the William Kennedy Smith case tried unsuccessfully to portray Smith as a premeditative date rapist. True premeditative rapists can experience full arousal only when they are violent, and as a result they can enjoy sex only when they force it. How their sexual and aggressive faculties combine to cause this restriction is the province of sexologists. Almost all men are capable of rape, including vast numbers who are conscious of this fact and never permit themselves to do it. But a few find that rape is the only sex they can have. Such men are dangerous. As date rapists, they work much as child molesters work with candy. The pleasantries of the date do not have value in themselves for them, but instead they are instruments, planned in advance or extemporized, to bring the victim to a setting convenient for rape. The rapist then moves so rapidly toward sex that most women would resist, and the resistance allows him to enjoy forcing sex upon the woman. If he is the kind of rapist who seeks to produce an orgasm in his victim, he may continue until the woman experiences a semblance of an orgasm, after which the victim sometimes is left troubled but confused, and unable to act decisively.[8]

Rapists have always existed and always will because the world is imperfect. Whether they can be "cured" is an issue for therapists. Their existence, however, does not betoken much of a trend. They have to be stopped; that is all. Failure to take seriously their offenses is itself a repudiation of privacy as a value. However, as the 1990s began a broad constituency in the United States took these offenses seriously, and the existence of this constituency is evidence that the right to privacy has strong endorsement.

Omitted from the discussion so far have been the less frequent forms of rape: stranger rape, male homosexual rape, female-to-male rape, and female homosexual rape. These are as bad as the more common forms in terms of invading privacy.

Stranger rapes remain probably the most terrifying. In stranger rapes, murder appears to be closer at hand. Perhaps premeditated date rape is not enough for some men because they must inspire terror as well as resistance if they are to enjoy themselves. The victim of a stranger rape is probably less confused than victims of other rapes, but she may be more fearful.

It is difficult to gauge whether male homosexual rape is rare or common. One associates it with prisons, where it appears to be common. Otherwise, it appears to be rare. Probably, it has not often been reported. Victims have not wanted to admit that they were subjected to it. Some victims probably have thought of it as just another way of being beaten up. As of the 1990s, an increase in reporting could be expected because due to the spread of AIDS, the high likelihood of transfering AIDS through anal intercourse, and the association of AIDS with homosexuality, rapes of this kind began to look like urgent life or death matters.

Although some people might challenge that it is ever possible for a woman to rape a man, at least one such case has reached the courts.[9] Paradoxically, such experiences, at least for a young man, might turn a victim into a rapist himself. Apparently, men who as children are sexually exploited by women tend to become sexual assaulters of women.[10] With this thought in mind, one might ask whether the experience of rape turns women toward later criminality. Clearly, female rape victims do not often resort to rape themselves. Yet one might look to see whether they in any way visit retaliatory invasions of privacy upon men or upon other women.

Where the original offense is an invasion of privacy, the retaliation is in kind as long as it is an invasion of privacy, even if it is not rape. Maybe all rapes fall in a cycle of reciprocating invasions, the rapist retaliating for a childhood invasion of a different order, such as the refusal of parents or guardians to provide him with room to grow—for example, by discouraging a talent of which they did not approve—or such as a single painful invasion, for example, when a parent or older sibling reads a truly secret diary. The rape then converts the victim to the cycle of invasions, and she retaliates against men or against other people in general by reading a child's diary, by violating someone's request to be treated with respect, or by breaking a confidence by publicly disclosing an extremely embarrassing fact about someone. Then the person invaded, male or female, retaliates with invasions of a different kind, perhaps making up rumors to damage a reputation or simply never being willing to let another person sit quietly and read. Eventually someone in the cycle returns to rape as the instrument for invading privacy.

Rapes can also be discussed with the focus on victims. The important questions are different. They include the following: How long did it last? Was it physically brutal? Was it mentally brutal? Was it terrifying? Did you come out of it with a fighting spirit or were you crushed? Was it disorienting? Did you put the blame on yourself?

The answers to such questions create a set of categories, such as: long rapes, short rapes, brutal rapes, crushing rapes, confusing rapes. These categories do not mean much except with reference to the individual experiences of victims, with regard to whom they mean a great deal as personal ordeals.

One way to make sense of these ordeals is to look upon them as invasions of privacy. If anything suggests the importance of invasion of privacy as a concept, it is its helpfulness in understanding reactions to rape. It is helpful to third parties, and it should also be helpful to victims. The more comfortable a person is with talking about an invasion of privacy and in insisting that he or she has privacy that deserves respect, the clearer that person's understanding of rape will be, and the more aggressive will be the person's posture in protesting a sexual assault. For a victim, a sense of outrage that her or his privacy has been invaded should produce a clearer mind and a greater commitment to bringing about a moral symmetry—that is, finding and punishing the rapist.

The question for a confused or embarrassed victim never should be: Was I raped? The question always should be: Was my privacy invaded? If the answer is yes, if the invasion was sexual, and if it included physical contact, then a rape or sexual assault took place. The reason it often is not helpful to approach the offense through the concept of rape is that the term "rape" is freighted with sexual-property myths. The upshot of rape, in a traditional view that is still widespread, was understood to be the defilement of the woman. Defilement meant the woman's conversion into damaged property, so that she was no longer an item of quality merchandise for a husband or suitor to have, or for a father, mother, uncle, or brother to give or bargain away. If a woman uses this approach, she feels she had better keep the rape to herself, as though it were her own fault, in order to avoid rejection by those close to her. Because of such baggage, rape as a concept does not suggest a clear course of action for victims.

However, when rape is recognized as an invasion of privacy, the course is clearer. The damaged-goods implications of a rape become irrelevant because, privacy being a personal right, the only important damage to be recognized becomes that to the victim personally.

Not everyone is ready to approach rape in this way. Some still think victims are damaged property. Others are troubled by the pleasure factor and are reluctant to acknowledge a rape when the attacker manages to produce an orgasm or any sensation of pleasure in the victim.[11] Victims are not accustomed to thinking in terms of privacy, and therefore are often unable to objectify their own need for privacy as a concrete component of themselves. As a result, they often are unable to realize that the sensation they experienced—not the feelings but the sensation—the alienation from one's own body, the sense of needing to wash, is the mind's reaction to an invasion of privacy and is, all by itself, something to arouse anger.

Many people have begun to accept that a rape occurs whenever sex proceeds over a woman's assertion of "no,"—or a man's protest—and that this is not acceptable. So, as of the 1990s, the message of rape—that privacy is important and rape is a glaring symbol of an invasion of privacy—is available to be read by anyone who has eyes to read it.[12]

NOTES

1. According to the 1990 FBI *Uniform Crime Reports*, forcible rapes nationwide rose from 34 per hundred thousand in 1982 to 41.2 per hundred thousand in 1990. *The World Almanac and Book of Facts 1992.*

An analysis of FBI *Uniform Crime Report* figures from 1970 to 1980 by Larry Baron and Murray A. Strauss, *Four Theories of Rape in American Society* (New Haven, CT: Yale University Press, 1989), indicates rapes per hundred thousand increased in the West from 20 to 42 from 1970 to 1980; in the South from 18 to 33; in the North Central states from 15 to 26; and in the Northeast from 10 to 22.

2. Rape, it should be noted, is sometimes a crime of orgasm, not merely a crime of penetration. That is, a rapist's objective is sometimes not only to break into the sexual organs of an unwilling woman to satisfy himself with his own orgasm, but also to produce an orgasm in the woman against her will. As a result, some rapists will not release a victim until she has had an orgasm; and, given enough attention, some women's bodies will produce an orgasm, even as their minds resist—not a happy orgasm certainly, but enough to send the rapist home and to leave the woman feeling soiled to the quick and embarrassed about herself. See the statement of "Julio" in Les Sussman and Sally Bordwell, *The Rapist File* (New York: Chelsea House, 1981), pp.

45–56. It is no wonder that rape victims hate to hear police investigators ask them if they experienced an orgasm. On the one hand, the question reminds them of the event. On the other, it makes what may seem to the woman to be the nub of the offense sound like evidence of consent. Yet, it is an important question and often must be asked. In some contexts, the victim's orgasm will suggest consent; in others it will give a clue to the nature and pattern of the rapist. The motive of some rapists to produce an orgasm in the victim is a tip-off that domination through invasion of privacy is a major constituent of rape. Because the traditional definition of rape is penetration by a penis, some of the more modern terms, such as sexual assault, may be more appropriate because this offense can be committed without penetration yet can be as bad as traditional rape.

3. The makers of the 1980s movie *Ghostbusters* coined a useful term for this experience: slimed. The feeling that you have been slimed is the sensation that results when your privacy is invaded. In mild form, it is something everyone must put up with occasionally. In severe form, it can break you, at least for a moment.

4. The time limits for filing a sexual harassment suit under Title VII of the federal Civil Rights Act of 1964 are 180 days, or 240 days if a suit must first be filed with a state or local agency. Title VII suits are filed with the Equal Employment Opportunity Commission. 42 U.S.C.A. sections 2000e–2000e-17.

5. This distinction runs through U.S. Supreme Court rulings on the First Amendment, particularly in the area of obscenity. A nutshell synopsis of rulings in this area from the late 1950s to the 1990s is that only the most extreme pornographic statements can be penalized because words are thoughts not actions and thoughts cannot be subjected to sanctions. See *Roth v. U.S.*, 354 U.S. 476 (1957); *Memoirs v. Massachusetts*, 383 U.S. 413 (1966); *Miller v. California*, 413 U.S. 15 (1973); *New York v. Ferber*, 458 U.S. 747 (1982). Also, the McCarthy era of the 1950s ended with a U.S. Supreme Court ruling that made a similar distinction between thoughts as expressed in words and thoughts expressed in actions. The McCarthy era was made possible by Supreme Court decisions between 1950 and 1957 that endorsed the penalizing of thoughts as expressed in words favorable to communism. In *Dennis v. U.S.*, 341 U.S. 494 (1951), the U.S. Supreme Court ruled that the clear and present danger test did not require the government to wait to the last minute before stopping a threat to itself, but could act in advance when perception of the threat was reasonable; and therefore that punishment under espionage laws for advocacy of communist doctrine was permissible under the First Amendment. In

1957 the Court ruled that advocacy of communist doctrine could not be punished, although incitement of violent action could be. In *Yates v. U.S.*, 354 U.S. 298 (1957), the U.S. Supreme Court ruled that abstract advocacy of doctrine was distinguishable from incitement of violent action, and that only the latter could be punished consistently with the First Amendment. Going back even farther, one can find that the punishment of speech has, since nearly the start of the century, been restricted to only those situations in which speech is intimately linked to action. This is what the famous clear and present danger test, announced in a U.S. Supreme Court ruling in 1919—*Schenck v. U.S.*, 249 U.S. 47 (1919)—means: Words cannot be penalized unless they are on the very cusp of producing action menacing to life and limb. That words are likely to produce such action, or that they can reasonably be understood to threaten such action, or that they reasonably can be expected to produce such action, is not enough to justify a penalty; the words must not only create a reasonable expectation of such action, but they must also be a hair's breadth—or in 1990 terms, a fraction of a nanosecond—from bringing the action into reality.

6. According to a 1987 study by M. P. Koss, *Hidden Rape: A National Survey of Psychopathological Consequences*, Progress Report, 2RO1MH31618-04, to the National Institute of Mental Health, reported in Andrea Parrot and Laurie Bechhofer, editors, *Acquaintance Rape* (New York: Wiley, 1991), 15 percent of college women had been victims of forced intercourse and 4 percent of college men had participated as perpetrators.

7. Katie Roiphe, "Date Rape's Other Victim," *New York Times Sunday Magazine* (June 13, 1993); 26.

8. See the statement of "Julio" in Sussman and Bordwell, *The Rapist File*, pp. 45–56.

9. *State v. Stevens*, 510 A.2d 1070 (Maine 1986). See also the opinion in *People v. Liberta*, 485 N.Y.S.2d 207 (1984). See also the statement of "Zeke" in Sussman and Bordwell, *The Rapist File*, pp. 29–43.

10. See statement by "Zeke" in Sussman and Bordwell, *The Rapist File*, pp. 29–43.

11. See the statement of "Julio" in Sussman and Bordwell, *The Rapist File*, pp. 45–56.

12. In terms of the discussion in Chapter Four regarding types of privacy, rape is a violation of privacy as a limitation on access to ourselves and of privacy as a demand for respect. In terms of the reference in Chapter One to the invasion of privacy using recognized legal categories, rape is a severe example of invasion of privacy by physical intrusion. If the rapist were clothed with governmental authority, as

a police officer, judge, or executive official would be, rape technically also would be a violation of the constitutional privacy right, even though no criminal penalties or civil causes of action have directly rested on the constitutional right.

Chapter 8

News-Reporting Ethics

Laws cannot solve all problems involving invasions of privacy. For mass media organizations, the ethical standards of practitioners and of the organizations themselves are more important than legal curbs might be. During the 1990s a variety of news-reporting intrusions have been prominent among invasions of privacy: reporting the names of sexual attack victims, reporting about victims of other crimes and of disasters, grief reporting, and reporting on the private lives of celebrities. All four could be corrected by changes in the ethical standards applied in reporting.

The above four intrusions are distinct from the large class of gray-area news invasions. With regard to gray-area invasions, reasonable arguments can always be made that asserted invasions are not actually invasions, or that, even if they are, no sound public policy can place on them a value higher than that of the people's need for disclosure. News-reporting intrusions that fall in this gray area include reports on medical problems of political figures; reports on domestic problems of those who trade on being celebrities; background reports on those drawn into public arenas, such as witnesses called to appear in notorious trials; or photographic attention to random persons on the street because they embody themes in an article to be illustrated by means of the photos. Many news-reporting intrusions cannot be remedied: reports on President Dwight Eisenhower's heart, President Ronald Reagan's bullet wounds and colon, and President George Bush's thyroid. The public clearly needs the information involved.

The four intrusions listed previously are different. The reporting of sexual assault victims' identities is a true invasion. Advocates for victims argue that disclosure of victims' identities compounds the pain of the assaults themselves. One way the pain is compounded is that disclosure exposes victims to scrutiny and sympathy, both of which they often find to be offensive. Moreover, victims perceive that satisfaction of public curiosity about their identities essentially provides titillation to some readers, viewers, or listeners and, as a result, generates an extra layer of sexual exploitation. Some people even blame the identified victims for the rapes.[1]

These concerns are understandable to most decision makers in the news business and are translated at most news organizations into policies against disclosing the identities of sex crime victims. These policies represent unpressured ethical action by news executives for court rulings establish that the media has a constitutional right to publish victims' names, provided the names do not come from sealed court documents.[2]

By 1990, some executives in the news field were arguing that in concealing victims' names, the media were conspiring to endorse an old myth that being a rape victim is shameful and were, as a result, frustrating the development of an openness that might bring about more prosecutions, more convictions, and fewer assaults.[3] This was indeed a persuasive argument because bold women, bounding back aggressively from sexual attacks, would indeed make a difference.

However, tampering with one's private parts is as private as the parts are themselves, and broad distribution of the facts of such tampering is at least as invasive of privacy as publishing pictures of one's private parts. The reason private parts are called private parts is because we crave privacy regarding them and the uses for which they are designed. As a result, if something is sexual, it calls out for privacy even if it is a crime that can be punished only in public proceedings. If a matter is essentially private, it can rightly be made public only with the consent of the person who holds the right to claim the privacy. Arbitrarily making public what the privacy holder declines to reveal jeopardizes everyone's privacy, and there is no way to argue around the fact that sexual assaults create a reasonable desire in the victims for privacy.

As a result, the prosecutorial benefits of open identification of sexual assault victims can be pursued rightly only by trying to convince victims to go public. The choice must be theirs. Because most news executives have given the choice to the victims, the form of news intrusion represented by identification of such victims has rarely occurred during the 1980s and 1990s.[4]

The problem of sexual assault victims' identities is the tip of an iceberg of similar problems. These are the problems that arise when that which is public is not entirely public. Neither news ethicists nor lawyers nor legislators like to wrestle with anything so intermediate or troubling, but if public proceedings following a rape must in part be kept private in deference to victims, then reporting on other public proceedings may have to be curtailed to protect other privacy interests. The message delivered by a rule against reporting rape victims' names is that court-related and courtroom activities may be totally open to those who can attend court or visit the courthouse, but they cannot be handled as totally open to those beyond the courthouse who are listeners, readers, or viewers of mass media reports. The message is that the scope of mass media publicity itself creates a new order of invasion simply because of its scale. For this reason, it can damage an individual's right to privacy, even when what is reported are public proceedings guaranteed by the Constitution in order to protect other individual rights. To repeat, the large scale of mass media publicity turns public proceedings into invasions of privacy. This is what the rule protecting sexual assault victims' names means. Or, differently put, court proceedings are supposed to be public, but not *that* public.

According to the same principle, other legal business that must be perfectly open and public in the courthouse might be subject to an invasion of privacy when spread far by the mass media. Following the international broadcasting of the William Kennedy Smith trial in the fall of 1991, some members of the public asserted that the trial should not have been televised, that the spotlight was turned too boldly on a range of people, including witnesses and attorneys, that something undesirable happened when the jury in the open courtroom was vicariously joined by an audience of millions. In the same spirit, one might question whether court television should have been created, or ask that all courtroom broadcasts be edited with an eye toward protecting privacy.

Most of the material in the live televising of courtroom proceedings does not invade privacy. Criminal defendants cannot be afforded rights to privacy regarding court appearances or information presented in court that bears on their cases, even if they are later acquitted. For some witnesses, however, live broadcasting may invade their privacy. For example, subpoenaed witnesses may be cross-examined regarding their character or forced to disclose delicate facts about themselves. For such witnesses, the televisers might offer some privacy comparable to what news organizations provide for sexual assault victims.

From a legal standpoint, media organizations should receive precisely the same discretion that they get regarding rape victims' identities—an unqualified right to publish or broadcast the identity. However, following the ethical model established with respect to rape victims' names, the media should apply some ethical brakes to televising courtroom testimony.

This same principle might be used in yet other areas of court news reporting because such reporting does occasionally cause intrusions. For example, an elderly man or woman who survives a mugging but whose name, address, typical shopping itinerary, solo householding, living habits, and life-style are disclosed in news reports about proceedings against the mugger is egregiously deprived, for a time, of the privacy usually valued highly in later years and also is endangered as this information is made available to people even more criminal than the mugger.

Similarly, people victimized in confidence rackets are wounded when practically everyone they know, plus others, are informed that they were so stupid that they let themselves be deceived and looted. Similarly, women beaten by boyfriends, wives beaten by husbands, men beaten by girlfriends and husbands beaten by wives are invaded when every acquaintance they have is told about the ugly interior of their intimate relationships. Sometimes such victims are key players in public life and details must be reported because they are essentially political items. When they are not key players, the reporting may be nothing more than gratuitous or accidental exploitation of the legal requirement that court proceedings be open.

Reporting on civil cases can present some of the same problems, occasionally in more severe form because the content of civil disputes, which are between private parties, is not as consistently demanding of public attention as that of criminal cases, even though the process of court resolution in civil cases demands just as much scrutiny as that in criminal cases. A lawsuit against an automobile manufacturer to recover damages for injuries caused by an accident in an allegedly defective car may demand detailed reporting. Yet a dispute between a homeowner and a shrub dealer may not be a proper context in which to tell the community about one party's credit history.

Disaster reporting can produce news intrusions akin to those produced by court reporting. For example, a report on a fire at an elderly person's home can intrude on the victim's privacy by including the same disclosures noted in the hypothetical mugging example above.

Information about family relationships, medical history, therapy history, educational history, sexual preference, credit history, or income can come out in reporting on victims of disasters, including fires, road accidents, construction disasters, airplane crashes, explosions, floods, landslides, radiation leaks, tornados, derailments, electrocutions, bridge collapses, stadium panics, ferry sinkings, hurricanes, smog emergencies, bear attacks, or drownings. Sensitivity to the privacy of people who have had public scrutiny visited upon them literally by accident might encourage some reporters to extend a degree of choice to these people. Extending choice is essentially what the rule against publishing sexual assault victims' names does.

Grief reporting also can cause intrusions. Much of the effort put into print and electronic news stories during the 1990s has been to capture drama in crises, and reporters are alert for emotional displays of any kind. Hence, television viewers often see tears shed at happy reunions, expletives hurled in confrontations, and sometimes shoulders racked with sobs. Reporters are instructed to interview survivors, the parents, or the family.

Reporting on happy tears may be justifiable as striking a positive note, and reporting about angry confrontations is often needed to define a political controversy, but grief reporting can be simply unconscionable. It is a violation of privacy as control over others' access to information about ourselves, of privacy as a safety valve, of privacy as room to grow, and of privacy as respect. However, in practice the situation is not so simple. Reporters discover that under conditions of grief, some people like to talk, or need to talk, publicly, about the grief, the disaster, or the person lost. As a result, the reporter may actually become a comforter of the grieving. When this happens, the element of exploitation vanishes, and with it the invasion of privacy. The practical challenge for the reporter, then, is to gauge whether or not he or she represents a comforter to the potential interviewee. This is not much of a challenge. It is met by asking the person if he or she wants to talk. If the response is "no," the reporter must retreat if no invasion of privacy is to occur. The model is almost identical to that of date rape. A "no" must be respected if an invasion is to be avoided. The "no" must be respected even if the reporter feels pressure from editors or colleagues back in the newsroom.

Asking a simple question and honoring a negative answer if it comes, will work as well for a television reporter with camera crew as it will for a solo print reporter. Once people signal that they would like to talk publicly, tears that follow come within a cooperative framework created by the speakers' choices. Only when the speakers indicate that they cannot continue, or obviously become unable to continue, must the reporter's attention and camera be turned away. However, the proper starting question is "Would you like to talk publicly about this?" or "Would you like to talk to us about this?" or something similar; it should not be "Are you willing to talk to the media?" or any other phrasing that is centered on the media's need or greed for the quotes or the footage. Reporters should merely offer an opportunity to the aggrieved to seek a moment's solace in making public comments. Any benefit the media may receive must be derivative of the service provided the aggrieved. The media's benefit cannot be primary in the minds of reporters, and ethical reporters must have the fortitude to stake their promotions on maintaining this attitude every time out. The most satisfactory solution would be for editors and news directors to support reporters in maintaining this attitude.

Grief reporting, then, can be egregiously invasive of privacy, but the invasions easily can be avoided through questions by reporters that are geared in a straightforward way to sensitivities that reasonably can be understood to exist in many people in extremis. In practice, though, this means that cameras cannot be turned upon people collapsing under the blow of tragic information and that reporters must wait for early paroxysms to pass before asking anyone if he or she would like to talk publicly.

Another area in which news reporting has disregarded privacy has been in reporting on the private lives of celebrities. These invasions could be addressed legally through modifications in the tort lawsuit for public disclosure of embarrassing private facts. This lawsuit has frequently been attacked as moribund,[5] but it might be strengthened rather than discarded. This strengthening would require a change in the "unconscionability" test through court recognition that disclosures regarding the private lives of celebrities may offend community standards of decency.[6] Such a change would pit privacy interests squarely against First Amendment press interests.[7]

However, an ethical solution is available to the problem, eliminating the need for a legal one. Journalists must recognize that public lives have private sectors and that sensitive reporting in these private sectors would send out the badly needed general message that privacy is important. Journalists have had no trouble in the past recognizing the value of privacy. For example, the alleged sexual peccadillos of John F. Kennedy, Lyndon B. Johnson, Robert F. Kennedy, and Martin Luther King were not reported at the time. Franklin D. Roosevelt went through several terms as president without the public being particularly aware that he used a wheelchair. Newsreels and early televised images were restricted to occasions when he was behind a desk or podium or, as in the famous photo of him at Malta with Stalin and Churchill, sitting down. Also, the public did not know that he had a mistress to whom he was sincerely attached. The press discussed neither matter. In addition, journalists in the last decades of the century have indicated that they too know how to protect privacy, but typically they have done this in the context of honoring promises to keep the identity of news sources confidential. For example, Bob Woodward and Carl Bernstein, the reporters on Watergate for the *Washington Post*, have resisted for twenty years all efforts to persuade them to reveal the identity of Deep Throat, their chief informant when they were handling the Watergate story.

These court, disaster, grief, and celebrity intrusions are not only true invasions of privacy but are also symptomatic of an era. Sexual assaults are forceful as ugly symbols because as physical invasions of privacy they are concrete. As sexual invasions they touch a personal base of understanding in a third party, and as vivid invasions they communicate a hint of the victim's sensation of being soiled and revolted. They are strong symbols of physical invasions of privacy and of all invasions of privacy. News-reporting intrusions are not this forceful but are symbols nevertheless—of another kind of invasion of privacy, though not of all invasions—intrusions on information access control.

Intrusions on information access control characterize the late twentieth century and threaten to characterize the twenty-first. They are the invasions made possible by advances in record-keeping technology, in speed of information transfer, in the technology and methods of surveillance, and by the willingness of most people to volunteer personal information to data banks so that they can get credit easily. They are the types of invasions that the federal Privacy Act of 1974[8] was meant to address by limiting the movement of information contained in government dossiers, and which universities sought to protect by prohibiting the posting of grades by social security numbers. These are the kinds of invasions that can occur as information leaks out in the processing of medical insurance claims, during credit checks, and in police investigations.

Arguably, it was this kind of invasion of privacy that alone sharpened the public's sensitivity to privacy. Historically, privacy gathered importance in the second half of the twentieth century. The preceding half century was marked by the growth of efficient surveillance, computer-based record keeping, and an expansion of scale among private and governmental organizations that found it necessary to keep track of their members, constituents, employees, and beneficiaries in order to effectively provide services and maintain order.[9] The sensitivity to privacy that makes rape seem to be a doubly horrible offense as the twenty-first century approaches may have been born in the uncomfortable awareness that too many people, some in powerful positions, know too much about each of us—in part because we ourselves have traded privacy for services.

It is the discomfort of living in an information fishbowl that news-reporting intrusions symbolize. We have to put up with having our lives detailed in tax, police, medical, insurance, education, and credit data banks; on top of this, the news media will not give us room to cry alone when we are sad, or to buy groceries and go to the bank without the whole community being informed of our habitual itineraries, or to come to terms with flood damage without being made an object of the public's capricious sympathy. This is what some people have started to feel.

As a result, even though news-reporting intrusions occur only infrequently, they have acquired an importance out of proportion to their frequency. This challenges news organizations to reduce the frequency even further and points toward a better mass media, one more sensitive to what is and is not an invasion of privacy. Yet it will never be easy for the mass media to make this ethical step forward because, quantitatively, the reduction of invasions in privacy through reporting inevitably results in a reduction in the sum total of information circulating. Of course, the quantitative loss can promptly be offset through increased reporting on essential non-private matters, which will result in a qualitative gain.

NOTES

1. See David A. Kaplan with Elizabeth Ann Leonard, "Should We Reveal Her Name?" *Newsweek* (April 2, 1990); 48. Allan Siegel, *New York Times* assistant managing editor, is quoted as saying, "This victim stands accused of nothing and this society would find it repugnant to add to her obloquy." Geneva Overholser, editor of *The Des Moines Register*, is quoted as saying that only in sex crimes do victims "risk being blamed in so insidious a way—she asked for it, she wanted it."

2. See *Cox v. Cohn*, 420 U.S. 469 (1975).

3. The best-known supporter of this position was Geneva Overholser, editor of the *Des Moines Register*. See David Margolick, "A Name, a Face and a Rape: Iowa Victim Tells Her Story," *New York Times* (March 25, 1990), I, 1:1.

4. A few news organizations identified the complaining party in the William Kennedy Smith rape case of 1991. Most did not. Following the conclusion of the trial, she volunteered her identity to the public. At that point, all news organizations carried her name.

5. Randall P. Bezanson, " 'The Right to Privacy' Revisited: Privacy, News, and Social Change, 1890-1990," *California Law Review* 80 (1992); 1133; Harry Kalven, "Privacy in Tort Law—Were Warren and Brandeis Wrong?" *Law & Contemporary Problems* 31 (1966); 326; Diana L. Zimmerman, "Requiem for a Heavyweight: A Farewell to Warren and Brandeis's Privacy Tort," *Cornell Law Review* 68 (1983); 291.

6. A public disclosure of an embarrassing private fact cannot be the basis of a damage judgment unless it is "unconscionable," a standard most famously recognized in a lawsuit won by the *New Yorker* in 1940, *Sidis v. F-R Publishing*, 113 F.2d 806 (2d Cir. 1940), and defined in the *Sidis* case as revelations "so intimate and so unwarranted in view of the victim's position as to outrage the community's notions of decency."

7. It would challenge the tradition of regarding those who accept public figure status as having also accepted public and press scrutiny of their private lives, a tradition recognized in *Sidis v. F-R Pub-*

lishing, 113 F.2d 806 (1940), in which the favorable ruling for the magazine defendant resulted from the court's observation that the plaintiff, aggrieved at having been reported to be destitute, had been a public figure since childhood, when he had received national recognition as a mathematics prodigy. The tradition has been explicitly constitutionalized by the U.S. Supreme Court since then in libel and false light invasion of privacy rulings, which reduce the availability of damages in these lawsuits when the plaintiffs are public figures, that is, have acquired fame or notoriety in their communities, have placed themselves in the limelight at least regarding limited issues, or have accumulated enough status so that they can demand and get access to mass media through which to reply to the criticism. See *Gertz v. Welch*, 418 U.S. 323 (1974). See also *New York Times v. Sullivan*, 376 U.S. 254 (1964), *Curtis v. Butts*, 388 U.S. 130 (1967), *Time v. Hill*, 385 U.S. 374 (1967).

8. 5 U.S.C.A. 552b.

9. See Vance Packard, *The Naked Society* (New York: D. McKay, 1964); James Rule et al., *The Politics of Privacy* (New York: Elsevier, 1980).

---------------- Chapter 9 ----------------

Invasions of Privacy

Sexual assaults and harrassment account for no more than a small fraction of invasions of privacy. Similarly, news-reporting intrusions by the mass media account for no more than a small fraction. Privacy has been threatened or violated regularly in other ways during the middle and late twentieth century. We have not recognized some of these threats or violations as such, so commonplace are they. We do not give them a thought. Yet they are invasions, and we do notice them occasionally. At times—for example, while providing personal information to a banker or a census taker—a person might think, "I guess they know everything about me." There is little anyone can do about some invasions; they are the price paid for credit or governmental assistance.

Among the threats to access-control privacy are the following:

1. Government access to bank information such as canceled checks, statements, credit cards, or electronic fund transfers.[1]

2. Leakage through the medium of criminal records, which are open unless sealed, of information collected in criminal investigations, not only from people charged with crimes but also from others interviewed by investigators strictly as information sources, including confidential disclosures of personal information; disclosures required by subpoena from accountants, hospitals, banks, insurance companies, or employers; and information gathered in warranted searches.[2]

3. Distribution of consumer credit records and investigation reports.

4. Compilation of employment records, including health records and resumes, and the release of information contained therein.

5. Census and military files.

6. Sale of mailing lists, which imparted a socio-economic and buying-habit profile.

7. Medical records, over which control can be lost as a result of laws requiring doctors to report certain diseases, and medical insurance claims and employee medical records. The claims and records of necessity pass through many hands.

8. School grade records, which usually are available to all administrators and faculty.

9. Abuse of social security numbers by the curious who learn of another's number and, posing as the other, obtain facts about the other.

10. Leaks as a governmental agency's files are shared with other agencies.

11. Tax records, which can be reviewed by many when they are submitted in requests for loans or grants, for example, to cover educational expenses.

12. Intelligence quotient and other test records and counseling records from high schools and universities.

13. Surveillance measures available to police agencies

that produce information about a person outside the concerns that justified the surveillance. These measures include taps and bugs, including mail taps, bumper beepers, and infrared viewers.

The invasion of access-control privacy concerns a broad range of people. Such invasions are as distasteful to highly gregarious extroverts as they are to reclusive introverts. It is the type of invasion most seriously threatened by the technology of surveillance and record keeping. During the last half of the twentieth century, computers, particularly the networks of powerful governmental computers and of comparable tools in the financial industries, have increased substantially the thoroughness with which access-control privacy can be invaded. Widespread sensitivity to this threat has resulted in legislation aimed at controlling invasions of access-control privacy by the major record-keeping organizations, principally the government. Nearly all of the privacy laws passed—except the few outlining a tort right and the few constitutional provisions describing a generalized privacy right—were directed at access-control privacy. For many people, access-control privacy is the whole of privacy.

Other kinds of privacy have continued to be threatened and violated. Invasions of respect privacy bring insults to the physical person or to symbols of the person. Violations may cause shame or at least embarrassment. An extreme violation of respect privacy is rape, in which a victim's sense of personal integrity is breached. Threats to respect privacy include the following:

1. Unwanted physical contact, as on crowded commuter trains or buses.
2. Toxic chemicals in food, water, or air.
3. Medications prescribed without explanation of side effects.
4. Aggressive photographers.
5. Use of polygraphs in employment settings.

Some violations of access-control privacy also damage respect privacy. Bugs and taps, for example, may generate information that violates access-control privacy while insulting the home, which is a symbol of the people who live in it.

Certainly many violations of respect privacy cannot be redressed, but a community that ignores privacy as respect causes more discomfort than is necessary and gives up some of the latitude it might need in order to get away with invading privacy when it must.

Respect privacy is violated by eavesdropping, which also invades access-control privacy. It is violated by a related offense that occurs, for example, when officers at civil service desks conduct business in voices loud enough to be heard throughout a room. Such invasions of respect privacy also violate access-control privacy. Respect privacy can be violated even by careless expectations by friends or acquaintances, that you will be open about your finances, your children's problems, or the causes of your divorce.

Arguably, a neighbor's cooking food outdoors at a time when the wind blows the smoke into your window invades your privacy as respect; the neighbor is, in effect, saying that your discomfort does not matter. Of course, redressing this invasion may not be worth the effort—may not even be fair in view of what you do to the neighbor.

Privacy as room to grow is less tangible than access-control or respect privacy. Violations of it are hard to identify. Sexual abuse of a child invades the child's room-to-grow privacy; so does violent child abuse. These two are clear violations. However, other violations are less clear, for example, when other family members pester a person who needs a little solitude, or a quiet college student is assigned to a rowdy dormitory.

Invasions of privacy as room to grow occur frequently, but they rarely justify organizational sanctions. They are the results of accidental or deliberate unkindness, from one person to another.

Privacy as room to grow has its clearest instrumental usefulness at schools, where students need to be alone in order to learn. No new wave of invasions threatens. By and large, the problems of schools are perennial ones and schools have established a degree of mastery over them. It is only at degenerating or degenerated secondary schools that the erosion of privacy as room to grow can be clearly seen as a feature of overall decay; these are the overcrowded urban schools at which students cannot find quiet moments inside the buildings to compensate for the absence of solitude everywhere else in their lives.

Some identifiable threats to privacy as room to grow are noise; verbal harassment; unpartitioned offices or living spaces; smoke, odors, and the results of poor ventilation; the non-stop schedule; unmonitored small children; aggressive conversational probing into personal problems; and physical trespasses, although trespasses are more typically violations of respect privacy. Laws or regulations have cured some of these threats; others have been cured by the resolve of the victims not to let the violations happen again.

This is a kind of privacy that means more to introverts than to extroverts, and therefore is very important to only a minority of people. If it ever erodes to the point where little learning is possible or where many find they cannot retreat often enough to handle personal crises, then a majority might become sensitized to it. However, in the late twentieth century most people usually have enough room to grow. The exceptions are celebrities.

Privacy as safety valve is not clearly under attack. Retreats from business and professional environments are available. For most people, safety-valve privacy does not require solitude. It is another kind of privacy with strong appeal to extroverts and therefore potentially commands the backing of a majority. Many still find it possible to retreat into their families or with close friends, confident that their behavior in these select groups will not be exposed to public view or reported to those who might seek reprisals.

Many activities can satisfy this need for privacy as safety valve: a dinner with family, a poker game with friends, a car trip with friends or family, a talk with one's minister, a quiet morning alone fixing the plumbing or car, a training run with other runners. Opportunities abound to escape from unpleasant people, to mock them with abandon, to say what you really think of management, of the philanderer on the board, of the colleague with bad breath.

The sense of security with which one can indulge in safety-valve privacy is threatened in a few ways. Unpartitioned offices lessen the availability of such privacy in the middle of the day. The non-stop schedule wipes out the opportunity altogether. Trespasses invade this privacy. But these dangers are not so common as to generate serious concern. Most people are not bugged or tapped. Many offices are partitioned. The people with non-stop schedules have only themselves to blame. Trespasses by eavesdroppers or private investigators are infrequent. As a result, safety-valve privacy appears to be secure.

The fear that safety-valve privacy could be lost has been cresting periodically into public discussion for about forty years. George Orwell's novel *Nineteen Eighty-Four*[3] effectively made the point that when safety-valve privacy is lost, all privacy is gone, and the ability to invest oneself in personal aspirations or in love dies with it. As a result, safety-valve privacy, by whatever name, has importance as a litmus. It is the last in the line of dominos; when it is gone, personality is gone. Technology, in theory, has the power to wipe out personality.

However, as the century draws to a close safety-valve privacy does not appear to be under attack. Big Brother is not yet watching. On the contrary, this kind of privacy appears to be healthy. Its apparent health may have lulled some people into thinking that all privacy is secure and may account for why more people are not actively concerned about threats to the access-control or respect types of privacy.

Clearly, only a fraction of privacy violations can be stopped. Some of those that occur regularly are not worth the effort required to prevent them, for example, the distribution of school grade records. Others are parts of procedures in which the benefits outweigh the risks to privacy: turning over tax records in order to get grants or loans for college; building consumer credit records in order to get credit; or taking psychological tests in order to get more accurate career counseling. Other invasions cannot be prevented because they have to be balanced against other rights or interests.

That many invasions cannot reasonably be addressed or must be regarded as secondary to other interests does not mean that the invasions do not occur. Life is filled with invasions, and these accumulate and rankle even though many of them are beyond reach. The best that can be hoped for as the turn of the century approaches is a change of attitude that would reduce the frequency of violations to a minimum and a change of policy that would make a few more of them addressable. Most people probably are more interested in preventing the further loss of ground than in gaining any.

NOTES

1. See William R. Petrocelli, *Low Profile: How To Avoid the Privacy Invaders* (New York: McGraw-Hill, 1981).

2. Ibid.

3. George Orwell, *Nineteen Eighty-Four* (New York: Harcourt, Brace, 1949).

Chapter 10

Summary

In our information age, privacy is threatened by surveillance technologies, data management, and mass media, but also by the goal these technologies serve. The goal is to promote social problems over private and public problems, with a blurring of the distinction between private and public as a consequence. The goal is a feature of changes in work life. From the mid-nineteenth century on, these changes have made the problems of production, labor relationships, socio-economics, distribution of wealth, dynamics of class, conflict of ethnic groups, and international trade competition the chief concerns of public policy and decision making. Previously, these were the private concerns of family enterprises, business houses, and banks, while the public concerns of governments were wars and the propagation of political ideals. Generally, these changes in the world of work improved the lives of many, but by 1950 a clear distinction between public and private had been lost.

People in the United States and elsewhere need privacy as much as, or even more than, ever before because the process of etherealization, as described by Arnold Toynbee,[1] has carried them forward to a point where their continued success and survival requires that they meet interior, almost spiritual, challenges, for which privacy is a facilitator and symbol. As the century ends, people need privacy as much as they needed freedom of speech during the eighteenth century. Many people have become consciously aware of this need and have begun to resist social science surveys and governmental surveys such as censuses. They have started to complain that agencies of government and business collect more information than they need. They have acquired some sense of offense, mixed with continued fascination, about mass media probes into the lives of public persons and demands for statements from victims and survivors. Not all steps have yet been identified that might strengthen privacy, keep it secure, and prevent it from overrunning other important interests.

NOTE

1. According to Toynbee, the challenges a society must meet in order to survive become increasingly "ethereal," ceasing to be challenges on the level of taming prairies for planting, making the desert bloom, or winning wars, but instead becoming challenges to individuals to make themselves better persons. Arnold J. Toynbee, *A Study of History*, vol. 3 (New York: Oxford University Galaxy Book, 1962), pp. 174–192.

Selected Bibliography

BOOKS

Altman, Irwin. *The Environment and Social Behavior: Privacy, Personal Space, Territory, Crowding*. Monterey, CA: Brooks/Cole, 1975.

Arendt, Hannah. *The Human Condition*. Chicago: University of Chicago Press, 1958.

Banfield, Edward. *The Unheavenly City*. Boston: Little, Brown, 1970.

Blumstein, Philip, and Pepper Schwartz. *American Couples*. New York: William Morrow, 1983.

Bok, Sissela. *Secrets*. New York: Pantheon, 1982.

Briggs, Jean L. *Never In Anger*. Cambridge: Harvard University Press, 1970.

Cohen, Yehudi A. *The Transition From Childhood to Adolescence*. Chicago: Aldine, 1964.

Flaherty, David. *Privacy in Colonial New England*. Charlottesville: University of Virginia Press, 1972.

Fussell, Paul. *Class*. New York: Ballantine, 1983.

Hall, Edward T. *The Hidden Dimension*. New York: Doubleday, 1966.

Herman, Judith Lewis. *Father-Daughter Incest*. Cambridge: Harvard University Press, 1980.

Hixson, Richard F. *Privacy in a Public Society*. New York: Oxford University Press, 1967.

James, Henry. "The Private Life." *The Novels and Tales of Henry James*, New York Edition, Vol. 17. New York: Kelley, 1970.

———. "The Reverberator." *The Novels and Tales of Henry James*, New York Edition, Vol. 13. New York: Kelley, 1970.

Keirsey, David, and Marilyn Bates. *Please Understand Me*. Del Mar, CA: Prometheus Nemesis, 1984.

Kroger, Otto, and Janet M. Thuesen. *Type Talk*. New York: Delacorte, 1988.

Lyons, William E. *The Disappearance of Introspection*. Cambridge: MIT Press, 1986.

Meares, Ainslie. *The Introvert*. Springfield, IL: Thomas, 1958.

Moore, Barrington, Jr. *Privacy*. Armonk, NY: Sharpe, 1984.

Myers, Isabel Briggs. *Gifts Differing*. Palo Alto, CA: Consulting Psychologists Press, 1980.

Norman, Jane, and Myron W. Harms. *The Private Life of the American Teenagers*. New York: Rawson, Wade, 1981.

Orwell, George. *Nineteen Eighty-Four*. New York: Harcourt, Brace, 1949.

Packard, Vance. *The Naked Society*. New York: D. McKay, 1964.

Petrocelli, William R. *Low Profile: How to Avoid the Privacy Invaders*. New York: McGraw-Hill, 1981.

Pratt, Walter F. *Privacy in Britain*. Lewisburg, PA: Bucknell University Press, 1979.

Rawley, James A. *The Transatlantic Slave Trade*. New York: Norton, 1981.

Reynolds, Edward. *Stand The Storm*. New York: Allison and Busby, 1985.

Rule, James, et al. *The Politics of Privacy*. New York: Elsevier, 1980.

Schneider, Carl D. *Shame, Exposure and Privacy*. Boston: Beacon, 1977.

Shils, Edward. *Center and Periphery: Essays in Macrosociology*. Chicago: University of Chicago Press, 1975.

Slough, M. C. *Privacy, Freedom and Responsibility*. Springfield, IL: Thomas, 1969.

Smith, Robert Ellis. *Privacy*. Garden City, NY: Archer/Doubleday, 1979.

Storr, Anthony. *Solitude*. New York: Free Press, 1988.

Toynbee, Arnold J. *A Study of History*. volumes 7, 8 and 9. Oxford and New York: Oxford University Press, 1963.

Updike, John. *Rabbit Redux*. New York: Knopf, 1971.

Westin, Alan. *Privacy and Freedom*. New York: Atheneum, 1967.

Whitworth, John M. *God's Blueprints: A Sociological Study of Three Utopian Sects*. Boston: Routledge and K. Paul, 1975.

ARTICLES

Barnet, Richard J. "After the Cold War." *The New Yorker* 65, no. 46 (January 1, 1990): 65–76.

Chapman, John W. "Personality and Privacy." In J. Roland Pennock and John W. Chapman, *Privacy*. New York: Atherton, 1971.

Clausen, Christopher. "A Decent Impersonality." *The American Scholar* 54, no. 4 (1985): 537–540.

Gavison, Ruth. "Privacy and the Limits of Law." 89 *Yale Law Journal* 421 (1980).

Goyder, John, and Jean McKenzie Leiper. "The Decline in Survey Response: A Social Values Interpretation." *Sociology* 19, no. 1 (1985): 55–71.

Gross, Hyman. "Privacy and Autonomy." In J. Roland Pennock and John W. Chapman, *Privacy*. New York: Atherton, 1971.

Haviland, Leslie K., and John B. Haviland. "Privacy in a Mexican Indian Village." In S. I. Benn and G. F. Gaus, eds., *Public and Private in Social Life*. New York: St. Martin's Press, 1983.

Heckscher, August. "The Invasion of Privacy (2)—The Reshaping of Privacy." *The American Scholar* 28, no. 1 (1959): 11–20.

Kaplan, David A. with Elizabeth Ann Leonard. "Should We Reveal Her Name?" *Newsweek* (April 2, 1990): 48.

Jourard, Sidney M. "Psychological Aspects of Privacy." *Law and Contemporary Problems* 31, no. 2 (1966): 307–318.

McCloskey, H. J. "Privacy and the Right to Privacy." *Philosophy* 55 (1980): 17–38.

Margolick, David. "A Name, a Face and a Rape: Iowa Victim Tells Her Story." *New York Times* (March 25, 1990): I, 1:1.

Margulis, Stephen T. "Conceptions of Privacy: Current Status and Next Steps." *Journal of Social Issues* 33, no. 3 (1977): 5–21.

Murphy, Robert M. "Social Distance and the Veil." *American Anthropologist* 66 (1964): 1257–1274.

Negley, Glenn. "Philosophical Views on the Value of Privacy." *Law and Contemporary Problems* 31, no. 2 (1966): 319–325.

Newsweek (April 2, 1990): 48.

New York Times (March 25, 1990): I, 1:1.

Prosser, William. "Privacy." 48 *California Law Review* 383 (1960).

Reiman, Jeffrey H. "Privacy, Intimacy, and Personhood." *Philosophy and Public Affairs* 6, no. 1 (1976): 26–44.

Roberts, John M., and Thomas Gregor. "Privacy: A Cultural View." In J. Roland Pennock and John W. Chapman, *Privacy*. New York: Atherton, 1971.

Schwartz, Barry. "The Social Psychology of Privacy." *American Journal of Sociology* 73, no. 6 (1968): 741–752.

Shils, Edward. "Privacy: Its Constitution and Vicissitudes." *Law and Contemporary Problems* 31, no. 2 (1966): 281–306.

Spiro, Herbert J. "Privacy in Contemporary Perspective." In J. Roland Pennock and John W. Chapman, *Privacy*. New York: Atherton, 1971.

Steiner, George. "Literature and Post-History." In George Steiner, *Language and Silence*. New York: Atheneum, 1967.

———. "Night Words." In George Steiner, *Language and Silence*. New York: Atheneum, 1967.

Travers, Harold. "Orientation Toward Privacy in Hong Kong." *Perceptual and Motor Skills* 59 (1984): 635–644.

Van de Wetering, Maxine. "The Popular Concept of 'Home' in Nineteenth-Century America." *Journal of American Studies* 18, no. 1 (1984): 5–28.

Victor, Jeffrey S. "Privacy, Intimacy and Shame in a French Village." In Stanton K. Tefft, ed., *Secrecy: A Cross-Cultural Perspective*. New York: Human Science Press, 1980.

Vidmar, Neil, and David H. Flaherty. "Concern for Personal Privacy in an Electronic Age." *Journal of Communications* 35 (2) (1985): 91–104.

Warren, Carol, and Barbara Laslett. "Privacy and Secrecy: A Conceptual Comparison." *Journal of Social Issues* 33, no. 3 (1977): 43–51.

Warren, Samuel D., and Louis D. Brandeis. "The Right to Privacy." 4 *Harvard Law Review* 193 (1890).

Index

Authoritarian tendency, Germany and, 18
Autonomy, 48, 50, 53

Bank information, 121
Barnet, Richard, 87
Black Americans, 32–41
Blacks, 32–41, 85
Blumstein, Philip, 17
Bodily matters of an individual, government tampering with, 5
Bok, Sissela, 47, 50, 53
Books, 19
Boot camp, 55, 59 n.40
Bourgeoisie, 17, 20
Brandeis, Louis, 4
Briggs, Jean L., 11–12
Britain, 17–18, 48

Castle, home as, 17
Census, 24, 121–122
Certainty, privacy and, 76, 83, 88
Chapman, John R., 56
Chiapas, 13
China, 16
Christianity, 2, 16–17, 33
Civil law, 28 n.56
Class, 21, 39–40, 41–45, 84, 129
Clausen, Christopher, 25–26
Clothing, 21, 52, 84
Cohen, Yehudi A., 14
College campuses, acquaintance rape and, 98–99
Commercial exploitation of the individual, 3–4
Common law, 17–18
Commonplace invasions of privacy, 121–122
Complex obligations, disclosure of personal information necessitated by, 23–24

Compulsive informality, excess of, 25–26
Computers, 23, 40, 123
Confucian axiom regarding lust, power and greed, 84
Congregational tradition in America, 6
Constitutional privacy right, 5, 32
Control, privacy and, 49, 51
Counterculture of 1960s and 1970s, 56
Court proceedings, 111–113
Courtroom broadcasts, 112
Credit, 12, 32, 40, 113, 117, 121–122, 126
Criminal records, 122

Dangerous dogs, 13
Data banks, 22, 72
Date rape, 98–101
De facto sexual harassment, 96
Decay of the inner life, 25
Diaries, 15
Differentiated model of sexual identity, 97
Domestic privacy, 10
Doors, 10, 17, 18, 52, 55
Droit du seigneur, 1
Drugs, 84, 88
Dwellings, 10, 11, 13, 20–21

Egalitarian tendency, U.S. and, 18
Electronic data processing, 2
Emotional control, 78–79, 85–87
Emotional reticence, 11
England, 17, 18, 20, 22, 69
Eskimos, 11–12
Etherealization, Toynbee's concept of, 129